The Posture Triangle

A New Framework for U.S. Air Force Global Presence

Stacie L. Pettyjohn, Alan J. Vick

RAND Project AIR FORCE

Prepared for the United States Air Force
Approved for public release; distribution unlimited

The research described in this report was sponsored by the United States Air Force under Contract FA7014-06-C-0001. Further information may be obtained from the Strategic Planning Division, Directorate of Plans, Hq USAF.

Library of Congress Cataloging-in-Publication Data is available for this publication.

ISBN: 978-0-8330-8167-4

The RAND Corporation is a nonprofit institution that helps improve policy and decisionmaking through research and analysis. RAND's publications do not necessarily reflect the opinions of its research clients and sponsors.

Support RAND—make a tax-deductible charitable contribution at www.rand.org/giving/contribute.html

RAND® is a registered trademark.

Preface

Over the past several decades, the U.S. global defense posture has gone through two major realignments. The first, following the end of the Cold War, substantially reduced the number of overseas bases and returned thousands of troops to bases in the United States. The second, following the events of 9/11, expanded some overseas bases, created many new ones, and deployed close to 200,000 U.S. military personnel at the 2008 peak.

Now with the war in Iraq over and operations in Afghanistan winding down, the United States is entering another global posture realignment. The combination of war fatigue among the American population, fiscal constraints, and congressional concerns that U.S. overseas infrastructure may be excessive all are producing pressures to shrink the U.S. presence abroad.

On the other hand, there are limits to how much the United States can draw down if it wishes to remain a global power. Although the number of U.S. facilities and U.S. troop levels in Southwest Asia is slated to drop substantially over the next few years, the demands of ongoing counterterrorism operations in Southwest Asia and Africa as well as continuing tensions with Iran suggest an enduring, if smaller, U.S. presence in the region. At the same time, the growing U.S. focus on the Asia-Pacific region is creating new demands for a greater U.S. military presence. Finally, looking beyond these specific regional developments, there are several U.S. national security requirements that can be met only through sustained access to foreign soil.

To address these and related policy issues, RAND Project AIR FORCE conducted a multiyear assessment of the historical, regional, and global aspects of U.S. force posture. Analytic and policy findings of fiscal year 2011 study results are documented in

- Lynn E. Davis et al., *U.S. Overseas Military Presence: What Are the Strategic Choices?* (MG-1211-AF), 2012
- Stacie L. Pettyjohn, *U.S. Global Defense Posture, 1783–2011* (MG-1244-AF), 2012
- Alan J. Vick and Jacob L. Heim, *Assessing U.S. Air Force Basing Options in East Asia,* (MG-1204-AF), January 2013, not available to the general public
- Jeff Hagen, Patrick Mills, and Stephen M. Worman, *Analysis of Air Operations from Basing in Northern Australia* (TR-1306-AF), March 2013, not available to the general public.

Building on these earlier studies, RAND Project AIR FORCE conducted a fiscal year 2012 study under the sponsorship of the Vice Chief of Staff of the U.S. Air Force. This study sought to answer four fundamental force posture questions raised by the U.S. Air Force Chief of Staff:

1. Why does the USAF need a global posture?
2. Where does the USAF need basing and access?
3. What types of security partnerships minimize peacetime access risk?
4. How much forward presence does the USAF require?

This report presents a summary treatment of all four policy questions. Additional details on supporting scenario and force structure analysis can be found in Jeff Hagen and Jacob L. Heim, *U.S. Air Force Global Posture: Using Scenario Analysis to Identify Future Basing and Force Requirements* (RR-405-AF), forthcoming.

The research described in this report was conducted within the Strategy and Doctrine Program of RAND Project AIR FORCE as part of a fiscal year 2012 study "Whither the Main Operating Base? Toward a New Framework for Global Posture."

RAND Project AIR FORCE

RAND Project AIR FORCE (PAF), a division of the RAND Corporation, is the U.S. Air Force's federally funded research and development center for studies and analyses. PAF provides the Air Force with independent analyses of policy alternatives affecting the development, employment, combat readiness, and support of current and future air, space, and cyber forces. Research is conducted in four programs: Force Modernization and Employment; Manpower, Personnel, and Training; Resource Management; and Strategy and Doctrine.

Additional information about PAF is available on our website:
http://www.rand.org/paf

Contents

Figures

Tables

Summary

U.S. Air Force (USAF) global posture—its overseas forces, facilities, and arrangements with partner nations—is a study in contrasts. On the one hand, there are those major bases where combat forces have been permanently deployed since the end of World War II. These bases are characterized by superb infrastructure, a large USAF presence (typically including dependents), and a substantial force element (typically a wing headquarters and associated units). There were dozens of these bases at the height of the Cold War, but relatively few exist today. For example, as of October 2013 there are only seven fighter bases abroad: Royal Air Force (RAF) Station Lakenheath in the United Kingdom; Spangdahlem Air Base (AB) in Germany; Aviano AB in Italy; Osan and Kunsan ABs in South Korea; and Misawa and Kadena ABs in Japan. In contrast to the relatively small number of major bases concentrated in a few countries, the USAF has dozens of smaller facilities hosting other activities. For example, there are early warning radars, space tracking, and communication facilities, such as Thule AB, Greenland; forward operating locations (FOLs), such as Kandahar Airfield, Afghanistan; en route airfields for transportation aircraft, such as Yokota AB, Japan; and small USAF training detachments rotating through airfields, such as in Lask, Poland.

This global posture faces a variety of political, fiscal, and military challenges. Within the United States, the Cold War consensus in support of a large overseas presence has eroded, while a clear alternative vision has yet to emerge. Fiscal pressures led Department of Defense (DoD) leadership to propose another round of domestic base closings in 2012, but members of Congress made clear that reductions would have to occur abroad before they would support base closings at home. Key partners nations, such as the United Kingdom, Germany, South Korea, and Japan, all remain strongly committed to retaining U.S. bases, but the broader overseas political climate presents greater risks to access. Regime change, democratization, growing nationalism, and domestic politics in partner nations together have created a climate less conducive to the permanent deployment of large foreign military forces. Finally, on the military front, emerging adversary precision long-range strike systems, such as China's large conventional ballistic missile force, present significant threats to forward bases.

USAF leaders face significant choices as they adapt global posture to these new conditions. This report is intended to inform their deliberations on global posture by addressing four fundamental questions about USAF force posture:

1. Why does the USAF need a global posture?
2. Where does the USAF need basing and access?
3. What types of security partnerships minimize peacetime access risk?
4. How much forward presence does the USAF require?

To answer these questions, we pursued several lines of research. First, we developed a logical framework—the posture triangle—to link U.S. national security requirements to specific types of posture. Second, we assessed the utility of dozens of airfields to meet mission demands for nine diverse scenarios. Third, we integrated our results with analysis conducted in previous (FY 11) research for the USAF—which together cover almost 30 scenarios and over 600 airfields. Fourth, we developed a method to assess peacetime access risk. Finally, we used the posture triangle framework to offer insights on sizing USAF overseas forces. Our research findings are presented below, organized around the four posture questions.

Key Findings

Why Does the USAF Need a Global Posture?

U.S. geography and overseas territories convey significant military advantages, but they alone are insufficient to meet three critical U.S. security requirements: (1) maintain security ties to close partners and key regions, (2) create and sustain operational effects, and (3) sustain global military activities.

For the first requirement, since the end of World War II the United States has relied on some type of enduring military presence to maintain these ties to our closest partners. Although U.S. military presence at these "strategic anchors" will evolve and at times may be modest in size, there is a world of difference between an enduring presence and none. Returning U.S. forces home may be attractive in theory, but U.S. experience since World War II confirms that it is extremely difficult to accomplish reassurance, deterrence, and regional stability missions with forces based exclusively in the United States.

Regarding the second national security requirement, U.S. territory alone is insufficient to conduct sustained operations outside of the western hemisphere. Access to FOLs on foreign territory is needed to generate operational effects. This is true for all four services. With respect to USAF force structure, current aircraft designs lack the range and speed to conduct sustained global round-trip missions from U.S. territory alone. Even long-range bombers are dependent on aerial refueling for many missions, and there are significant limits to air refueling support conducted exclusively from U.S. soil. Future technological breakthroughs may change this conclusion, but aircraft expected to dominate USAF force structure over the next 20 to 30 years are highly dependent (either directly or indirectly) on access to forward facilities.

Finally, to sustain global military activities, access to foreign territory is necessary to host support links. The links—en route airfields, ports, logistics facilities, and communications and early warning sites—are all constrained by either the range and endurance of the forces they support or other geographically driven factors (e.g., for early warning radars). Figure S.1 brings together these requirements and activities into a conceptual framework that we call the posture triangle.

Figure S.1. The Posture Triangle

Forward Operating Locations

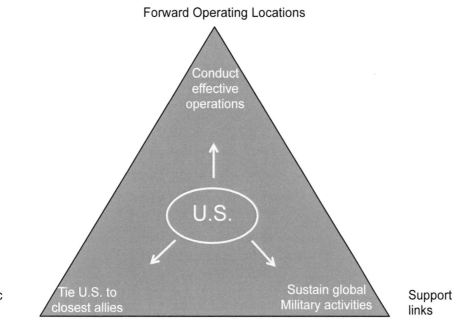

Strategic
Anchors

Support
links

Where Does the USAF Need Access and Basing?

Our analysis, which considered ongoing activities and operations, key relationships, and the demands of almost 30 diverse scenarios, identified 13 strategic anchor countries, 11 basing clusters, and 35 en route airfields as particularly valuable.

If we do some modest rounding, this analysis suggests a rough rule of thumb for planners: 12-12-36. That is, as the USAF plans for future demands on the force, it should expect to be called upon to maintain forces and facilities in up to a dozen strategic anchor countries, to have the capacity to conduct operations from FOLs in roughly a dozen basing clusters, and to require en route airfields in about three dozen locations. Although this may sound like a large posture, when compared with the past, 12-12-36 is relatively small (see Figure S.2). Moreover, the USAF peacetime presence at most of the en route locations is minimal, and there is no peacetime presence at most forward locations. Also, the specific demands on the USAF at these locations vary greatly.

Figure S.2. Major USAF Bases Overseas, 1953–2011

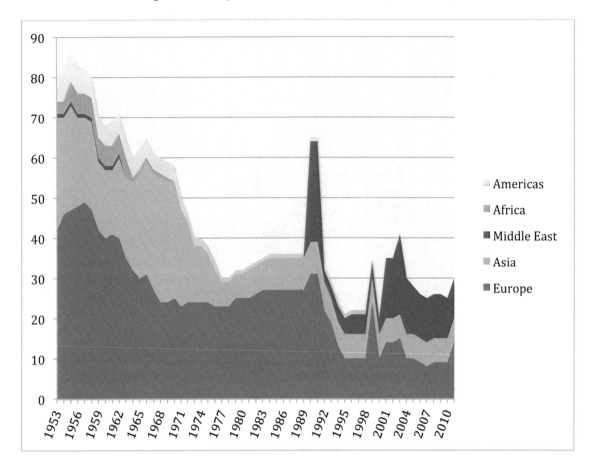

For example, where another service is not meeting U.S. strategic anchor needs, the USAF might deploy fighter aircraft; tankers; intelligence, surveillance, and reconnaissance (ISR) platforms; other capabilities; or a composite organization combining all these elements. FOL demands vary across missions and platforms. They may be met in some cases by existing airfields, whereas in others U.S. and partner nations may need to make selected investments in operating surfaces, parking, fuel systems, or other infrastructure. Finally, although the USAF requires a few high-capacity mobility hubs, such as Ramstein AB in Germany, the majority of locations in the current air mobility en route system place quite modest demands on USAF resources because they either have no permanent staff or the staffs are quite small. Additionally, most of these airfields are not owned or maintained by the USAF. They are either commercial, sister service, or partner nation airfields. This is a great bargain when the small investment in personnel is compared with the operational versatility and resilience that is gained from regular access to these facilities.

What Types of Security Partnerships Minimize Peacetime Access Risk?

This study developed an access risk metric based on regime type and the nature of the basing relationship. Domestic political institutions play a large role in a host nation's propensity to contest U.S. bases and access, with consolidated democracies the most dependable, nonconsolidated democracies less reliable, and authoritarian regimes the most problematic. Although regime type influences the reliability of peacetime access, other factors, including differing ideational motivations, strategic perspectives, and bargaining incentives, are key to understanding access risk.

We argue that a second variable—the type of access relationship—captures these different factors and significantly impacts the level of risk. Access relationships fall into one of three categories: a desire for material benefits (transactional), a shared perception of threat (mutual defense), or a deep security consensus (enduring partnership). In the transactional model, the host government makes bases on its territory available to secure material benefits in the form of rents, economic assistance, or arms sales. Compensation-driven access creates an unstable dynamic, because the host nation has every incentive to highlight problems associated with the U.S. presence to extract larger payments. A mutual defense relationship, in contrast, is built on a shared threat perception. This is a stable foundation for cooperation as long as the U.S. presence remains focused on countering the mutual security challenge. This is the most frequent reason nations give the United States access. In this relationship, however, the United States is likely to encounter difficulties if it tries to use its bases or forces for purposes unrelated to the mutual threat. The most stable relationship is the enduring partnership. The countries in this category all initially granted the United States basing rights for a reason (either shared threat or compensation) that has since disappeared. Yet, these nations continue to host U.S. forces because of an elite security consensus that the U.S. military plays a stabilizing role in the world and that the host nations have broad shared interests that are advanced by hosting U.S. forces.

We found that regime type and access relationship interact with one another and that particular combinations are especially stable or volatile. For instance, to date all of the United States' enduring partners have been consolidated democracies. Well-entrenched democratic institutions make it difficult for governments to modify or abandon existing basing agreements, while the shared identity fostered by a common form of government embeds U.S. access in a broader set of security cooperation activities. The second most durable type of access is based on a shared threat with consolidated democracies. Only one country in this category (France, 1966) has evicted U.S. forces, although the nature of post–Cold War relationships may make this somewhat more common in the future. By contrast, the least stable combinations involve authoritarian states that enter into transactional relationships with the United States. In this situation, dictators who are unfettered by institutional constraints can arbitrarily threaten to evict U.S. forces unless their terms are met. As a result, these relationships are unpredictable, and access is always in question. Autocrats who are interested only in compensation have entirely revoked U.S. access more than any other type of regime and access relationship.

How Much Forward Presence Does the United States Require?

It is much easier to identify the benefits of forward presence, both political and military, than to quantify how large a force is required to meet national security objectives. Deterrence, reassurance, and regional stability objectives are strongly tied to perceptions of U.S. capabilities and will. U.S. capability and will are both demonstrated through the forward deployment of forces that possess relevant capabilities in numbers that are generally recognized as significant. For example, a U.S. Navy (USN) carrier strike group, a U.S. Marine Corps expeditionary brigade, a U.S. Army brigade combat team, or a USAF wing are all widely recognized as significant combat formations and proof of a serious U.S. commitment to the partner. Where threats are more limited or there are political sensitivities, smaller deployments (e.g., a Patriot air defense battery or battalion) may meet such needs. That said, there is no authoritative means to show how variations in force size (e.g., adding or subtracting a few fighter squadrons) enhance or detract from these higher-level goals.

In contrast, theater campaign plan (TCP) requirements are readily quantified, and the effects of force size changes can be shown in theater combat simulations. Although this may appear to offer a means to size forward forces, in practice it is problematic. Because DoD and the military services use multiple "requirements" processes in force planning, there is a common perception that the type and size of permanently deployed forward forces is the product of such a process. That isn't quite the case. Campaign plan requirements change much more often than force posture does. Force posture is extremely resistant to change, due to the complex interplay of three factors: the U.S. planning, programming, and budgeting process; domestic political dynamics in both the United States and the host country; and the intricacies of negotiations between sovereign nations. For host nations, changes (whether expansion or shrinkage) in the type, size, and location of foreign forces have strategic implications: Enhancements may be viewed as provocative by some constituencies, while reductions may be seen by others as undermining deterrence. Major force changes also raise a host of local concerns about land use, safety, noise, and economic and social impacts. For these reasons, permanent force changes are usually relatively small, with large changes occurring only rarely. Given this reality, theater campaign planners can successfully make the case to retain forward forces because of their value but rarely can initiate major changes. Thus, forward force size is typically an input to rather than output of this process. To the extent that the TCP identifies additional force requirements, they would be deployed during a crisis period from the United States or other regions.

So how should the United States size forward forces? We suggest a multifaceted approach. First, where current forward forces can be shown as vital to meeting TCP requirements, they should be left in place. Second, where enduring partners show a strong desire to maintain current forces, DoD should seek to maintain a concrete symbol of U.S. commitment and capability, whether an Army or Marine Corps brigade, USAF wing, or substantial naval capability. The long-term benefits from these relationships greatly exceed the costs of maintaining what are now modest deployments. In these cases, the United States and the host nation should work together to evolve the forces and facilities in ways that are cost-effective in meeting both nations' security objectives. The USAF should expect a continuing demand for wing-size deployments in many strategic anchor countries. In some cases, a larger permanent presence will be called for; other partners (e.g., Australia) will prefer a smaller footprint. Third, DoD, combatant commands, and the services should explicitly embrace a capabilities-based approach in determining overseas force size. This approach would seek to identify key operational metrics to determine the type and size of forces desired in a given region. In some cases (e.g., U.S. European Command and U.S. Africa Command), forces based in one command might be the primary force provider for another.

Recommendations

- **Use an integrated framework to explain global posture.** Although DoD posture documents offer thoughtful, regionally based justifications for U.S. posture, elite opinion appears to be increasingly skeptical of such arguments. One possible explanation is the lack of an integrated framework for understanding global posture more broadly. Such a framework should explicitly demonstrate how specific elements of posture are needed to meet specific national security goals. We developed the posture triangle as a framework that can incorporate both qualitative and quantitative inputs and answer fundamental posture questions, ranging from "Why are we abroad?" to "How many bases are required?" The framework is intended to be a useful tool for both internal DoD planning and for public outreach. We recommend that DoD and the USAF either incorporate this framework into future posture documents and processes or develop their own approach. Either way global posture needs to be explained and justified within a framework that goes beyond arguments that are particular to a given country or region.
- **Maintain strategic anchor locations in key regions and with enduring partners.** An enduring U.S. military presence in key nations and regions contributes to regional stability, deterrence of potential foes, and reassurance of partners and allies. The size and type of presence should be tailored to the particular needs of the host nation and United States and may include one, some, or all U.S. services. In many cases, the permanent presence may be quite small, and in all cases rotational forces can (and do) supplement those permanently deployed abroad. We identify the United Kingdom, Germany, Italy, Spain, Japan, Korea, and Australia as top-tier strategic anchors—countries that have hosted permanent and often large U.S. facilities for 50 or more years. Kuwait, Bahrain, Qatar, and the United Arab Emirates are strategic anchor locations in the Persian Gulf and key partners in regional stability efforts. In Southeast Asia, Singapore has long hosted key USN logistics facilities and is now hosting USN littoral combat ships on rotational deployments. Finally, the Philippines, a Cold War–era strategic anchor for the United States, may once again play that role if current negotiations produce a new agreement that expands U.S. access to ports and airfields.

- **Expand access to potential forward operating locations in key regions.** During the Cold War, USAF bases such as Ramstein AB in Germany or Kadena AB in Japan played dual roles as FOLs and as part of the strategic anchor joint military presence. Today, we see FOL and strategic anchor demands diverging for two reasons. First, emerging long-range precision-strike capabilities in countries such as China and Iran will increasingly constrain use of the most forward bases as FOLs. Many bases that play vital roles as strategic anchors during peacetime may be limited in effectiveness during some phases of conflicts. This suggests a growing role for dispersal base FOLs to, at minimum, supplement forward bases during the most intense phases of combat. Second, existing strategic anchor locations are too few in number and too geographically concentrated to meet all U.S. needs for forward airfields. For example, there are no strategic anchors in Africa. To better prepare the USAF for potential operations across a wide range of scenarios, we recommend working with partner nations to identify and selectively develop FOLs in 11 "basing clusters." Most of these would have no enduring U.S. presence. Periodic small training visits or exercises with the host nation would typify the U.S. presence.

- **Use basing clusters to minimize access risk.** As noted above, the highest risk to peacetime access occurs when dictators provide access exclusively to receive compensation. These arrangements should be avoided except in extreme situations. That said, any purely transactional relationship (whatever the regime type) or access agreement with an authoritarian regime (even if mutual defense) is almost as risky. For this reason, U.S. planners should think of basing in terms of clusters—facilities that offer similar operational benefits but are spread across multiple nations. Likewise, U.S. policymakers should avoid publicly describing any particular facility or country as indispensable. Appropriate deference and appreciation can be paid to overseas partners without giving them undue power in facility access negotiations. Finally, basing clusters have the additional benefit of increasing operational resilience in the face of direct military threats to any of these airfields.

- **Expand USAF capability to support rotational forces.** Rotational forces have multiple benefits. Continuous rotational forces have proven to be an effective alternative in locations where a permanent U.S. presence is not politically viable. Periodic rotational forces are often used to supplement forward forces and to expand the range of capabilities available to theater commands. Since permanent force posture is difficult and slow to change (either up or down), rotational forces offer policymakers and commanders an agile policy instrument that can be used to support multiple policy objectives, including deterrent signaling and reassurance of partners.

    However, it is much more costly to rotate forces than to permanently base them abroad. In cases where a continuous presence is necessary, permanent basing will always be more cost-effective. Thus, continuous rotations should be minimized to the extent possible, recognizing that some critical presence missions can only be achieved this way. Where a continuous presence is not required, periodic rotations offer a means to exercise and train with partner nations, to improve infrastructure, and to demonstrate the ability to rapidly deploy to a region. The demand for periodic rotations is likely to grow from both partner nations and combatant commanders because of their political and operational flexibility. To support a growing demand for rotations, the USAF will need to develop new concepts to rotate forces more efficiently, receive additional resources, or engage in some combination of the two.

Global Posture for a Global Power

It appears that the debate about U.S. global posture has finally been joined. Much good can come from an open and thoughtful exploration of U.S. presence and access needs in the coming decades. Unfortunately, much of the current debate revolves around dangerous misperceptions. For example, some authors accuse long-time U.S. defense partners of freeriding on U.S. defense investments. Whatever the merits of arguments in favor of greater defense spending by particular partner nations, this line of argument misrepresents U.S. overseas military presence as one-sided, i.e., a gift to the host nation. In reality, these relationships have endured because of the considerable mutual benefits to both sides, including a wide range of security cooperation initiatives, increased regional stability, mutual support during contingencies, and, for the United States, the ability to conduct operations that would be infeasible without a global network of bases and partners. Americans take for granted the ability to project power globally, but this would not be possible without access to partner nation airfields, ports, and territory that often are not even in the immediate combat theater. For example, neither Operation Iraqi Freedom nor Enduring Freedom would have been possible without access to en route airfields and other support facilities in Spain, Italy, and Germany.

Another misperception is that great savings are to be found in cutting overseas forces and facilities. Most of the Cold War global posture has already been dismantled. Although some additional savings are likely possible, fiscal benefits must be carefully weighed against the operational and strategic costs. For example, the USAF has only seven fighter wings deployed abroad (one in the UK, one in Germany, one in Italy, two in Korea, and two in Japan), and only one of these (the 48th Wing at RAF Lakenheath in the UK) is a full wing. The remaining six all require reinforcements from the United States to be at full strength. With changing strategic demands, it is appropriate to consider whether some realignment is called for among overseas locations, both within and across regions. That said, any major realignment risks hindering opportunities for training with our closest partners, may undermine relationships that have provided benefits for many decades, and could lead to the closure of bases that have proven their worth in past contingencies. Fewer forces and fewer bases ultimately translate into reduced operational flexibility and could undermine U.S. regional stability, deterrence, and reassurance objectives.

Ultimately, the nation faces a critical choice: Do we intend to remain a global military power or not? There are substantial costs associated with either choice. If we choose the former, a large set of responsibilities and force demands flow from that decision and cannot be avoided. Global power necessitates a global force posture. It requires sustained and stable investment in human capital (our own and partners), forces, facilities, and relationships. These include developing and maintaining access relationships, forward bases, and forces; meeting security commitments to partner nations; sustaining a global transportation and communications network; and fielding forces capable of deploying globally and conducting effective military operations against a wide range of potential adversaries.

U.S. global posture is not the product of an overdeveloped sense of responsibility for other nations' security needs, but rather a prudent investment to protect U.S. interests. The fact that the United States has shared security interests with close partners in key regions is something to celebrate, not bemoan. The benefits in terms of opportunities for access and the ability to positively influence security in key regions far outweigh the costs of such commitments. That said, global posture should evolve to meet changing security demands, both in the nature and location of security threats. The future American global posture will feature a portfolio of arrangements and facilities, ranging from a small number of anchor bases in key nations to dozens of locations where its presence is modest and periodic. The Cold War global posture proved to be a strategic investment, serving the United States and its partners well for over 50 years. Current efforts to realign U.S. global posture into an increasingly agile and geographically diverse presence should likewise be viewed as a strategic investment, one that will pay benefits in ways unforeseen and over a time horizon likely measured in decades.

Acknowledgments

We thank General Philip Breedlove (then USAF Vice Chief of Staff) for sponsoring the study and Colonel James Casey and Mr. Lee Alloway (study project officers in Headquarters USAF, International Collaboration Group [AF/A5XX]) for their assistance during the study.

We also gratefully acknowledge the assistance of both leaders and personnel in the following organizations: Headquarters USAF, Headquarters Air Mobility Command, Headquarters Pacific Air Forces, 15th Wing, 515th Air Mobility Operations Wing, 154th Wing Hawaii Air National Guard, Headquarters U.S. Pacific Command, Headquarters U.S. Pacific Fleet, Headquarters U.S. Air Forces in Europe, 86th Airlift Wing, and the 521st Air Mobility Operations Wing. Mr. Steve Diamond, U.S. Pacific Command historian, provided access to manpower and facilities data essential for the historical analysis in this report.

At the Asia Pacific Center for Security Studies, we thank Lt Gen Daniel Leaf (USAF, ret.). At the Center for Strategic and Budgetary Assessments, we thank Evan Montgomery.

At RAND, we acknowledge the contributions of fellow project members Jeff Hagen, Jacob Heim, Stephen Worman (who conducted the geographic information system analysis and produced all the maps in this report), and Colonel Chuck Henderson (USAF RAND Fellow during 2011–2012). We thank Andrew Hoehn, Paula Thornhill, and Ted Harshberger for their enthusiastic support of this body of research and for their many substantive contributions to the key concepts in this report. Thanks also to Eric Peltz for his detailed comments and suggestions on the draft report. We acknowledge Judy Krutky of Baldwin-Wallace University for her contributions during her 2012 sabbatical at RAND, particularly her analysis of British and U.S. basing on the island of Diego Garcia.

Finally, we wish to thank Alexander Cooley of Barnard College and Paul Davis of RAND for their thorough and constructive reviews of this report.

Abbreviations

AB	air base
AFB	Air Force base
AMC	Air Mobility Command
COCOM	combatant command
DoD	Department of Defense
DPRK	Democratic People's Republic of Korea
FOL	forward operating location
FY	fiscal year
GIS	geographic information system
ISR	intelligence, surveillance, and reconnaissance
MCO	major combat operation
nm	nautical mile
ODS	Operation Desert Storm
OEF	Operation Enduring Freedom
OIF	Operation Iraqi Freedom
PACAF	Pacific Air Forces
PAF	Project AIR FORCE
ROK	Republic of Korea
TCP	theater campaign plan
UAE	United Arab Emirates
USA	United States Army
USAF	United States Air Force
USMC	United States Marine Corps
USN	United States Navy

1. Introduction

Background

Americans take for granted the global network of U.S. military facilities and forces stationed in many countries. Indeed, only those born prior to World War II have experienced a world where the United States did not have hundreds of overseas facilities and hundreds of thousands of troops stationed abroad.[1] Although there have been some recent calls for a dramatic reduction in our overseas presence,[2] a majority of Americans still support a continued military presence abroad.[3] This is unlikely to change anytime soon.

What is changing, however, are attitudes regarding the scale of the U.S. overseas presence. The Cold War elite consensus in support of large forces deployed at massive U.S. bases is gone. Although a new consensus has not yet emerged, it is clear that elite opinion is increasingly skeptical about the necessity for many overseas bases.[4] To the extent there is an elite consensus in 2013, it would maintain major facilities, such as Ramstein Air Base (AB) in Germany and Yokosuka Naval Base in Japan, but reduce or close others and return many U.S. forces home. Both Department of Defense (DoD) and outside commentators increasingly emphasize rotational deployments, and "places not bases" has become the guiding idea. For example, the 2012 DoD Strategic Guidance states that *"whenever possible, we will develop innovative, low-cost, and*

---

[1] In 1967, the United States had 1,228,538 troops stationed abroad and 1,014 facilities. In FY 2010, the United States still had 297,286 troops based abroad and 662 overseas installations (with 20 of them defined as "large sites" with real property value of at least $1.715 billion). See James R. Blaker, *The United States Overseas Basing: An Anatomy of the Dilemma*, New York: Praeger, 1990, p. 33; Defense Manpower Data Center, *Military Personnel Historical Reports, FY 1967*; Defense Manpower Data Center, *Active Duty Military Personnel Strengths by Regional Area and by Country*, September 30, 2010; Department of Defense, *Base Structure Report, FY 2010 Baseline*. For a history of U.S. global posture see Stacie L. Pettyjohn, *U.S. Global Defense Posture, 1783–2011*, Santa Monica, Calif.: RAND Corporation, MG-1244-AF, 2012.

[2] U.S. Representatives Ron Paul and Dennis Kucinich have both proposed withdrawing all U.S. forces from Japan. See "U.S. Reps Paul, Kucinich Urge Military Pullout from Japan Amid Budget Woes," *The Japan Times*, February 17, 2011.

[3] The Chicago Council on Global Affairs 2012 poll asked U.S. residents whether the United States should have more overseas bases, fewer bases, or about as many bases as we have now: 61% of respondents answered the same or more bases. See Chicago Council on Global Affairs, 2012.

[4] Examples include Defense Advisory Committee, *A New U.S. Defense Strategy for a New Era: Military Superiority, Agility and Efficiency: A Summary of the Findings of the Defense Advisory Committee*, Washington, D.C.: Stimson, November 2012; Mike Mochizuki and Michael O'Hanlon, "Solving the Okinawa Problem: How Many Marines Do We Still Need in Japan?" *Foreign Policy*, October 12, 2012; Barry R. Posen, "Pull Back: the Case for a Less Activist Foreign Policy," *Foreign Affairs*, Vol. 91, No. 1, January/February 2013; Benjamin H. Friedman and Justin Logan, "Why the U.S. Military Budget Is 'Foolish and Sustainable,'" *Orbis*, Vol. 56, No. 2, Spring 2012, pp. 179–183.

small-footprint approaches to achieve our security objectives, relying on exercises, rotational presence, and advisory capabilities."[5]

The Department of Defense has done a commendable job of first shrinking overseas posture following the end of the Cold War and then adapting it to support the massive demands of Operation Enduring Freedom (OEF) and Operation Iraqi Freedom (OIF) as well as U.S. Special Operations Command's expanded global role. Additionally, in the 2003/2004 time frame, DoD leaders and planners developed a more flexible and agile concept for basing that recognized the value, indeed necessity, of expanding U.S. access beyond its major bases in Europe and Northeast Asia.[6] Recent reports suggest that DoD is in the process of further reducing basing in Europe as part of a strategic "pivot" toward Asia.[7]

U.S. global defense posture—its overseas forces, facilities, and access arrangements with partner nations—is undergoing substantial, parallel changes: an increased emphasis on "places not bases," a strategic pivot toward Asia, the ramping down of combat operations in Southwest Asia, and reductions in the size of the U.S. forward presence in Europe. This emerging posture reflects much creative thought by the U.S. government, but global defense posture documents do not offer a compelling narrative that explains the contribution that U.S. global posture makes to American security. This report is intended to help USAF leaders contribute to that narrative by offering a framework that more explicitly ties elements of global posture to specific security objectives.

The Policy Problem

U.S. global posture in 2013 is the product of past conflicts, enduring threats (e.g., in Korea), and current operations. U.S. bases in Europe and Northeast Asia date back to the Cold War, Korean War, and World War II. U.S. bases in Southwest Asia date back to Operation Desert Storm, enforcement of no-fly zones over Iraq, or, more recently, to OEF and OIF. There are few current overseas bases specifically built to meet security challenges for the 2020s and beyond. That isn't to say that current posture is irrelevant to future needs, just that posture is deeply rooted in historical and current rather than future demands.

This is the core of the policy problem. How do we adapt and evolve a global network of facilities to meet the security needs of the future? What U.S. security objectives require overseas bases? Where do these bases need to be? What missions should these bases be ready to support?

---

[5] Office of the Secretary of Defense, *Sustaining U.S. Global Leadership: Priorities for 21st Century Defense*, Washington, D.C.: Department of Defense, January 2012, p. 3.

[6] See Ryan Henry, "Transforming the U.S. Global Defense Posture," *Naval War College Review*, Spring 2006, Vol. 59, No. 2, pp. 13–28; and Kurt M. Campbell and Celeste Johnson Ward, "New Battle Stations," *Foreign Affairs*, September/October 2003, pp. 95–99.

[7] Mackenzie Eaglen, "What's Likely in New Pentagon Strategy: 2 Theaters, Fewer Bases, A2AD," *Breaking Defense,* December 20, 2011.

What type and how large a force needs to be based abroad? What arrangements and relationships maximize access and minimize risk? How can DoD and the USAF sustain needed overseas presence in an era of intense global media coverage and scrutiny from domestic and international actors of U.S. overseas bases and security activities? In answering these questions, policymakers will need to keep in mind the evolving politics of access in an era characterized by growing nationalism on the one hand and increasingly integrated global information networks and virtual political movements on the other.

Purpose of This Document

This report provides an analytical foundation for USAF global posture deliberations, decisionmaking, planning, and external communication. It is intended to help USAF leaders and staff place USAF global posture in a broader historical and strategic framework, both to improve long-range planning and to better articulate the purposes and benefits of USAF overseas presence.

Organization

Chapter Two speaks to the question of why a global posture is needed. It describes the reach and limitations of military operations conducted from U.S. soil, identifies the reasons that the United States requires access to foreign soil, and presents the "posture triangle," a conceptual framework for organizing and explaining U.S. global posture. Chapter Three addresses the question of where the United States needs access, drawing on both the posture triangle and scenario analysis. Chapter Four seeks to answer the question "What types of security partnerships minimize peacetime access risk?" The chapter describes three models of basing relationships and presents a method to assess peacetime access risk. Chapter Five uses the posture triangle and a historical analysis to answer the question "How much forward presence does the USAF require?" Chapter Six presents conclusions and recommendations.

2. Why Does the USAF Need a Global Posture?

This chapter seeks to understand and identify the fundamental reasons for an overseas force posture. It begins with an exploration of the benefits and limitations provided by U.S. territory. It then presents a planning framework that illustrates how U.S. global posture addresses three core requirements.

The Reach and Limits of U.S. Territory

Any discussion of overseas posture ought to begin with an understanding of what can and cannot be accomplished from U.S. territory. As a continental power, the United States has great advantages. The lower 48 states offer unimpeded access to the waters and air of the Pacific, Atlantic, and Gulf of Mexico. Alaska and Hawaii also have immediate access to international airspace and seas and are stepping-stones to the Arctic and East Asia. USAF airlifters can launch from bases on the east coast and reach Europe without air refueling or stops. For example, from Dover AFB, Delaware, USAF C-17 transports can reach USAF bases in the United Kingdom, Spain, and Germany. From Elmendorf AFB, Alaska, C-17s can reach Korea or Japan. Similarly, from Eglin AFB, Florida, C-17s can reach most of South America without stops.[8]

When U.S. overseas territories are included, the potential reach of U.S. forces is greatly expanded. For example, a C-17 flying from Hawaii cannot reach the Asia mainland without air refueling or an intermediate stop. If, however, the C-17 launches from the American territory of Guam in the Marianas, it can reach all of Southeast Asia and Australia, most of China, and as far west as India.[9] Figure 2.1 illustrates one-way ranges from Guam for both the C-17 and the longer-range C-17ER.

Figure 2.2 displays U.S. territories. From west to east, they are Guam, the Commonwealth of Northern Marianas, Wake Island, Midway Atoll, American Samoa, Johnston Atoll, Palmyra Atoll, Hawaii, Alaska, the lower 48 states, Puerto Rico, and the U.S. Virgin Islands. As the map demonstrates, the extent of U.S. territory is vast: The distance from Cape Barrow, Alaska, in the north to American Samoa in the southern Pacific is more than 5,000nm; from Guam in the western Pacific to the U.S. Virgin Islands in the Caribbean is over 8,500nm.

---

[8] These calculations are conservative, using the Air Mobility Command (AMC) planning factor of 3500nm one-way unrefueled range for the C-17. See AMC, *Air Mobility Command Global En Route Strategy White Paper*, Scott AFB, Illinois: HQ Air Mobility Command, July 14, 2010.

[9] This assumes no overflight restrictions and uses the AMC 3500nm one-way trip planning factor. A C-17ER has a one-way range of 4400nm (per AMC planning factor), which would allow a flight from Guam to India with minimal overflight of other nations. For C-17ER one-way range, see "AMC's Pacific En Route Posture," briefing slides, Scott AFB, Illinois: HQ Air Mobility Command, January 2013.

Figure 2.1. C-17 Range from Andersen AFB, Guam

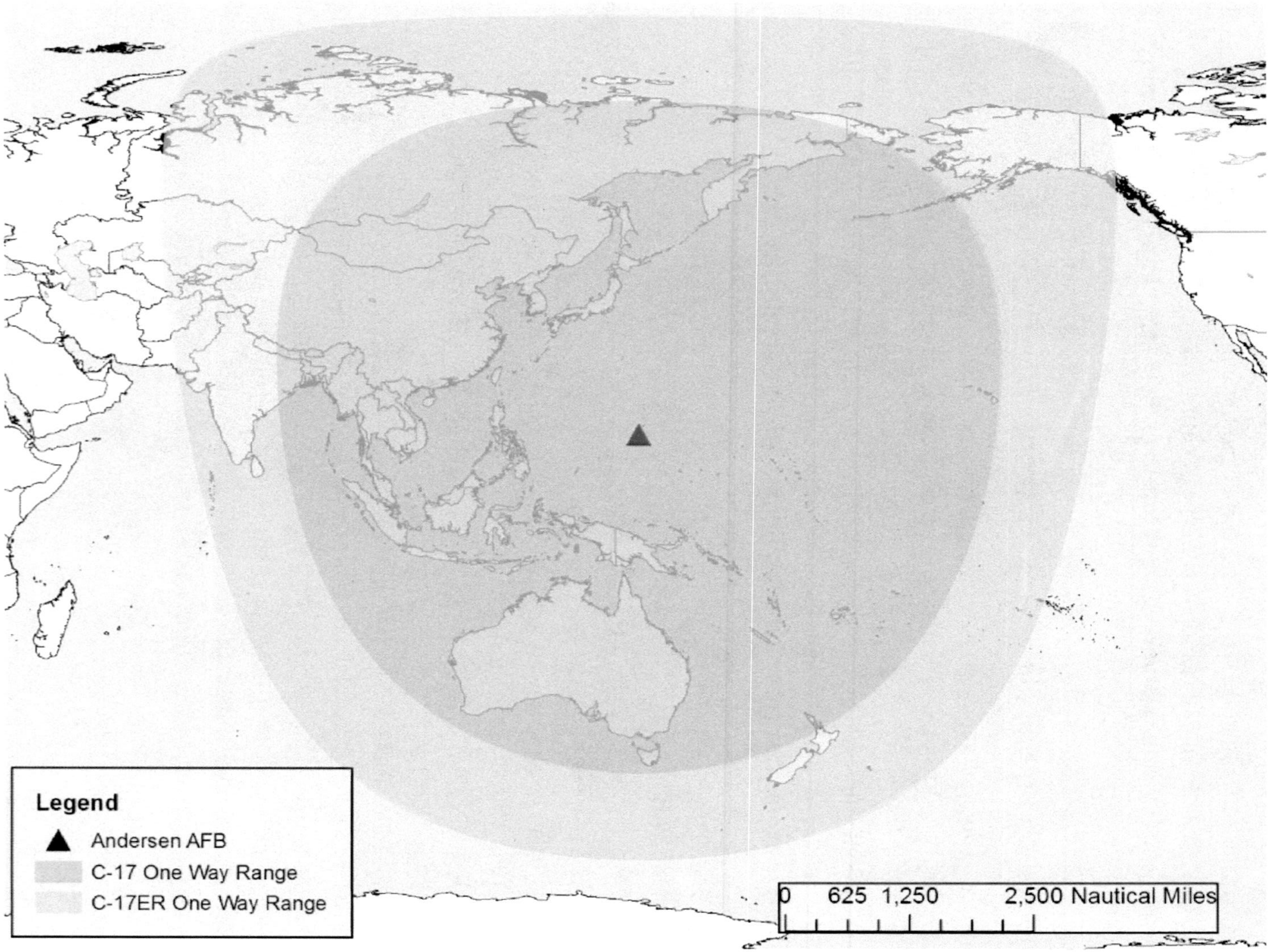

Legend

▲ Andersen AFB

C-17 One Way Range

C-17ER One Way Range

0 625 1,250 2,500 Nautical Miles

Figure 2.2. U.S. Overseas Territories

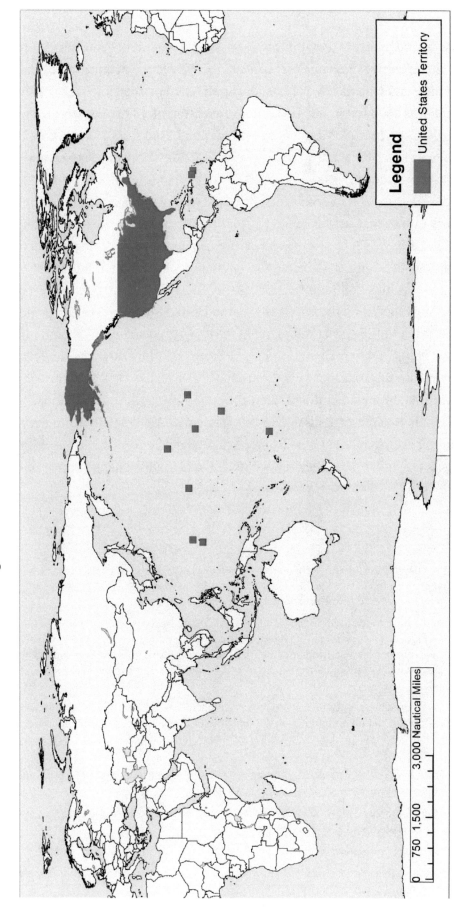

The United States acquired overseas territories during the 19th and 20th centuries. Midway was annexed in 1867. The Spanish-American War of 1898 resulted in the acquisition of Puerto Rico, Cuba, the Philippines, and Guam.[10] Wake Island was annexed by the United States in 1899.[11] American Samoa was acquired in the Tripartite Convention of 1899 (between Germany, Britain, and the United States). The U.S. Virgin Islands were purchased from Denmark in 1917. The Commonwealth of Northern Marianas, consisting of the islands of Tinian, Saipan, and Rota, was captured from the Japanese during World War II.[12]

The geography of the 50 states and overseas territories provide many benefits, but there are limitations to the military effects that can be achieved from American territory alone. From a military power projection perspective, U.S. soil is primarily of interest as the embarkation point for deployments and for logistical support. The number of major combat operations (MCOs) conducted directly from U.S. soil is quite limited. U.S. Army Rangers and the 82nd Airborne Division flew (on USAF airlifters) directly from bases in the United States to conduct combat airborne assaults into Grenada (during Operation Urgent Fury in 1983) and into Panama (during Operation Just Cause in 1989).[13] During Operation Desert Storm (1991), USAF B-52s flew round-trip combat missions from Barksdale AFB, Louisiana.[14] B-52s also flew from missions from the United States to Iraq during Operation Desert Strike (1996).[15] During Operation Allied Force (1999), USAF B-2s flew round-trip missions from Whiteman AFB, Missouri, to Serbia.[16] During Operation Enduring Freedom (2001), B-2s once again launched missions from Whiteman AFB. They flew to targets in Afghanistan, then landed in Diego Garcia to change crews and

---

[10] Cuba was an American protectorate from 1899 to 1902. The Philippines were under U.S. control from 1898 to 1946, when the Philippines were given independence. See George C. Herring, *From Colony to Superpower: U.S. Foreign Relations Since 1776*, New York: Oxford University Press, 2008, pp. 320–325.

[11] Other small uninhabited Pacific islands acquired by the United States include Baker Island, Howland Island, Jarvis Island, Johnston Atoll, Kingman Reef, and Palmyra Atoll. For more information, see U.S. Fish and Wildlife Service, "Pacific Remote Islands Marine National Monument." The United States also possesses one uninhabited island in the Caribbean, Navassa Island. For more information, see U.S. Geological Survey, *Navassa Island; A Photographic Tour*, 2000.

[12] See Herring, 2008, p. 257; Erik Goldstein, Richard Langhome, and Michael Graham Fry, *Guide to International Relations and Diplomacy*, New York: Continuum International Publishing Group, 2004, p. 154-156; John Constello, *The Pacific War: 1941–1945*, New York: Harper Perennial, 1982, pp. 484-486; and U.S. Central Intelligence Agency, *The CIA World Factbook: Virgin Islands*.

[13] See Mark Adkin, *Urgent Fury: The Battle for Grenada*, Lexington, Mass.: Lexington Books, 1989; and Edward M. Flanagan, Jr., *Battle for Panama: Inside Operation Just Cause*, Washington, D.C.: Brassey's, 1993.

[14] Bernard C. Nalty, *Winged Shield, Winged Sword: A History of the United States Air Force*, Volume II, *1950–1997*, Washington, D.C.: Air Force History and Museums Program, p. 460.

[15] U.S. Air Force, "B-52 Stratofortress," fact sheet, online, posted September 20, 2005.

[16] Office of the Secretary of Defense, *Report to Congress: Kosovo/Operation Allied Force After-Action Report*, Washington, D.C.: U.S. Department of Defense, January 31, 2000, p. 97.

refuel.[17] Finally, during Operation Odyssey Dawn (2011), B-2s once again launched combat missions from Whiteman AFB,[18] and USAF B-1s launched their first combat missions from the United States, making round-trip sorties from Ellsworth AFB, South Dakota, to Libya.[19] These are impressive missions and represent an important capability. That said, it should be noted that bombers were refueled during the missions by tanker aircraft flying out of USAF overseas bases and received overflight permission from multiple nations that sit between the United States and the target countries. Thus, these missions are not examples of purely autonomous operations from U.S. territory.

These examples demonstrate that deployments of light ground forces into Latin America or limited bomber operations at much greater distances are possible from U.S. soil—but are larger and more sustained combat operations feasible from U.S. soil? Consider contingencies in which the United States might wish to fly fighter missions from U.S. territory. For short periods of time, quite long-range missions might be envisioned, but for any conflict lasting more than a week or so, crew rest and other limitations constrain what is feasible. Figure 2.3 illustrates the area in which fighter operations might be sustained over an extended period. Such operations could cover all of North America, Central America and the Caribbean, northern South America, much of the Arctic, and virtually all of the northern Pacific. That said, vital regions are clearly not covered, including Europe, Africa, most of Asia, most of South America, Australia, and the southern Oceans/Antarctica. Looking beyond the USAF, the U.S. Navy (USN) can generate operational effects from carrier strike groups, submarines, and other naval assets in any littoral region, but it cannot sustain those effects without access to regional ports. In particular, USN vertical launch systems on its cruisers, destroyers, and submarines—which carry cruise missiles and other vital weapons—cannot be reloaded at sea. U.S. Marine Corps (USMC) and U.S. Army forces require forward logistical hubs to sustain operations that last more than a few weeks. In theaters where the United States had an enduring Cold War commitment (i.e., Europe and South Korea), the Army built a massive peacetime support infrastructure. For post–Cold War contingencies in Southwest Asia (e.g., OIF), the Army established large logistics hubs in the buildup to offensive operations. In both cases, large ground operations necessitated nearby support facilities. In short, all U.S. combat forces require access to foreign soil to either generate or sustain operational effects.

---

[17] One sortie lasted more than 44 hours, setting a new record for the longest combat air mission. See Benjamin S. Lambeth, *Air Power Against Terror: America's Conduct of Operation Enduring Freedom*, Santa Monica, Calif.: RAND Corporation, MG-166-1-CENTAF, 2005, p. 89.

[18] U.S. Air Force, "Global Strike Command Supports Operation Odyssey Dawn," Barksdale AFB, Louisiana: Air Force Global Strike Command Public Affairs, March 20, 2011.

[19] Hrair Palyan, *Lessons Learned, Operation Odyssey Dawn*, Ellsworth AFB, South Dakota: 28th Bomb Wing Public Affairs, March 21, 2012.

Figure 2.3. Nominal U.S. Fighter Aircraft Range from United States Territories

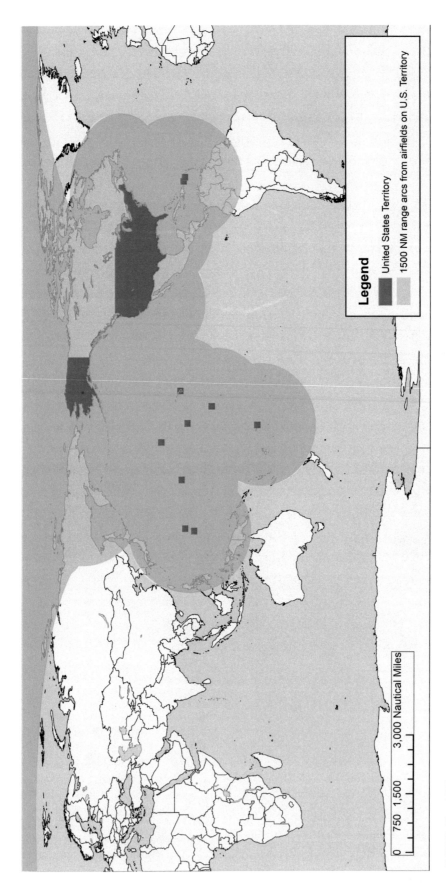

NOTES: The 1500nm range arcs were determined as follows. We assumed a 12-hour duty day (per AFI 11-202) with two hours devoted to preparation for each mission. This allows for 10 flight hours per day. At 450 kts cruise speed (with deductions for refueling at speeds closer to 300 kts) and a two-hour loiter on station, this results in an operating radius on the order of 1500nm. This is a very long sortie for a fighter and may be overly optimistic. Range arcs for U.S. states were measured from Barnes Municipal Airport (Massachusetts), Eglin AFB (Florida), March Field (California), Eielson AFB (Alaska), Point Barrow (Alaska), Savoonga Aiport (Alaska), Hickam AFB (Hawaii), and Eareckson Air Station (Alaskan Aleutian Islands). Other arcs were measured from U.S. territory on Guam, American Samoa, Palmyra Atoll, and the U.S. Virgin Islands. Thanks to project members Jeff Hagen and Stephen Worman for this analysis.

Conceptually, an inside-out approach is helpful in considering the range of basing options from U.S. territory to the most remote forward operating location (FOL) on foreign soil. As Figure 2.4 illustrates, we begin at the center with U.S. territory—the one place where access is guaranteed and U.S. military presence is permanent. Moving outward to the next circle, we come to U.S. overseas territory, where access and presence are high but a step below the 50 states. U.S. enduring partners offer the next level of access, with contingency and wartime partners at the bottom.

Figure 2.4. An Inside-Out Approach to Posture

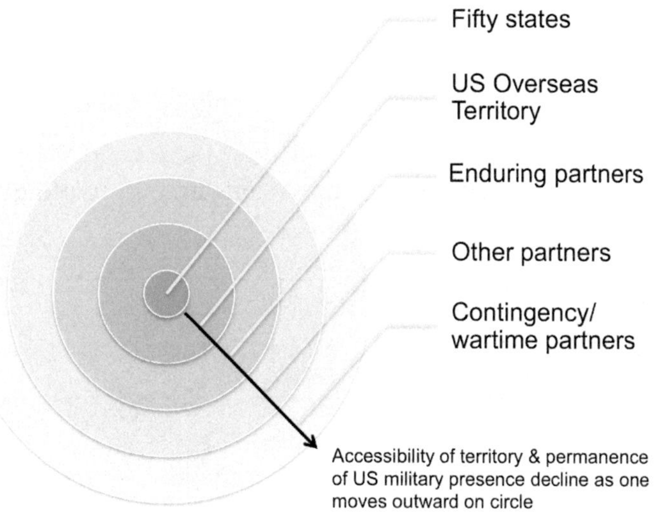

Fifty states

US Overseas Territory

Enduring partners

Other partners

Contingency/ wartime partners

Accessibility of territory & permanence of US military presence decline as one moves outward on circle

The Posture Triangle

Since the end of World War II, the United States has sought to protect its security interests through the projection of global military, political, and economic power. Projecting military power in peacetime (for deterrence and reassurance) and during conflicts generates three specific posture requirements:

- Maintain security ties to closest partners and key regions.
- Conduct effective operations.
- Sustain global military activities.

These three requirements can be met only through access to foreign soil. As we will discuss in more detail in the next chapter, an enduring military presence of some type has been integral to the relationships that the United States has enjoyed with its closest partners and has been a core component of U.S. regional security strategies. U.S. military facilities in the United Kingdom, Germany, Italy, Spain, South Korea, Japan, and Australia have been the foundation of

11

security cooperation with these close allies.[20] As a global power, the United States must also be capable of generating and supporting operations in key regions of the globe. To do this requires access to forward operating bases (FOBs), airfields, and ports in partner nations. As noted above, limited operations are possible without access to foreign soil, MCOs cannot be sustained in that fashion. Finally, a global power must have the means to enable military operations across vast distances. This requires communication and other support facilities as well as en route airfields and ports.

To support these needs the U.S. engages in three classes of activities:

- Create strategic anchors.
- Identify and develop FOLs.
- Maintain support links.

These activities align with the requirements listed above, as shown in Table 2.1.

Table 2.1. Overseas Military Requirements and Supporting Activities

	Strategic Anchors	FOLs	Support Links
Maintain security ties to closest partners and regions	X		
Conduct effective operations		X	
Sustain global military activities			X

Some facilities are associated with only one of these classes of activities, others with all three.[21] Ascension Island in the Atlantic is an example of a support link that is neither a strategic anchor nor an FOL. In contrast, Al Dhafra Air Base in the United Arab Emirates (UAE) can rightly be viewed as serving all three, acting as a strategic anchor for the United States, an FOL, and a support link (since it is a key en route airfield).

---

[20] Australia has not hosted large numbers of U.S. forces since World War II, but it has fought alongside American forces in every conflict since World War II, routinely exercises and trains with U.S. forces, currently hosts rotational USMC forces at Camp Robertson (near Darwin), and has provided U.S. forces access to its airfields, training ranges, and ports for decades. There also are joint U.S.-Australian military facilities, such as the Joint Defense Facility at Pine Gap and the Harold E. Holt Naval Communications Station. See *Joint Defense Facility at Pine Gap: Agreement Between the United States of America and Australia* signed at Canberra, June 4, 1998; Australian Department of Defence, "Australia-U.S. Joint Combined Training Centre," July 8, 2004; Joel Fitzgibbon, "Minister of Defence Meeting with U.S. Secretary of Defense, Signing of Harold E. Holt Treaty," July 18, 2008; and *AUSMIN 2010: Australia–United States Exchange of Letters Relating to Harold E. Holt Naval Communications Station,* November 8, 2010.

[21] Our framework is not a basing taxonomy that divides overseas facilities into mutually exclusive categories the way that DoD's system classifies facilities as either main operating bases, cooperative security locations, or forward operating sites. Such taxonomies are useful but are not particularly helpful in explaining *why* we need a particular facility. Our framework focuses on the relationship between activities at a site and national security demands.

Strategic Anchors

Since the end of World War II, prolonged threats to friendly nations in Europe, Southwest Asia, and East Asia led the United States to develop special relationships with key partners in each region. Nations who became close partners and who hosted some type of enduring U.S. military presence we describe as strategic anchors. The U.S. military presence is tailored to the needs of the United States and the partner nation. It may be small or large and composed of elements from any or all of the military services. Although nations who have hosted major force deployments (e.g., Germany, United Kingdom, South Korea, Japan) immediately come to mind, a strategic anchor need not host combat forces or large numbers of forces. For example, Bahrain is a strategic anchor in the Persian Gulf, yet until recently the U.S. presence there has been modest, primarily a USN headquarters and some support facilities. Australia is another example of a strategic anchor where the U.S. presence (until recently) included no combat forces but rather vital communications and related facilities. In all these cases, the U.S military presence in the strategic anchor country helps accomplish some or all of the following goals: fulfill security commitments, strengthen relationships with allies, and secure regional interests. Former Under Secretary of Defense Michele Flournoy and former Deputy Assistant Secretary of Defense Janine Davidson describe the purposes and benefits of an enduring forward presence:

> Aiming to prevent conflict, build the capacity of key partners, maintain core alliances, and ensure the U.S. military's ability to secure American interests in critical regions. . . . The cornerstone of forward engagement will be positioning U.S. troops in vital regions, particularly in Asia and the Middle East. As the long-term U.S. deployments in Europe and Asia have demonstrated, the physical presence of military forces sends a powerful message to potential adversaries.[22]

Oftentimes, a strategic anchor is used to underpin a U.S. security commitment to an ally. The presence of American forces, which are vulnerable to the same threats as the host nation, bolsters the ally's confidence in the United States' pledge to defend it from attacks. At other times, when a partner is relatively secure, a strategic anchor connects the United States to its ally and facilitates defense cooperation by helping to build and sustain relationships and enabling frequent security cooperation activities. Finally, strategic anchors may be established in vital regions where a continuous U.S. military presence is needed to deal with persistent threats to critical American interests.

One of the first strategic anchors was created during the Berlin Crisis of 1948, when the United Kingdom allowed U.S. B-29 bombers to indefinitely deploy to RAF bases.[23] Peacetime basing of U.S. forces overseas, however, did not become prevalent until fears of communist expansion soared after North Korea invaded South Korea in June 1950. Most European and

---

[22] Michele Flournoy and Janine Davidson, "Obama's New Global Posture: The Logic of U.S. Foreign Deployments," *Foreign Affairs,* Vol. 91, No. 4, July/August 2012, pp. 55–56.

[23] Simon Duke, "U.S. Basing in Britain, 1945–1960," in Simon W. Duke and Wolfgang Krieger, *U.S. Military Forces in Europe: The Early Years, 1945–1970,* Boulder, Colo.: Westview Press, 1993, pp. 125–128.

Asian states, however, had been badly weakened by World War II and were not capable of deterring the Soviet Union or its allies on their own. Consequently, nations threatened by communism had little choice but to align with the United States and permit the establishment of American bases on their territory.[24]

Due to the fact that the Cold War was a long-term competition with defined front lines, the strategic anchors established during the 1950s and 1960s were characterized by a large, permanent U.S. military presence largely consisting of major combat units (e.g., divisions, fighter wings, carrier battle groups). Moreover, because of the extended deployments required during World War II and for occupation duties, in the mid 1940s DoD began to allow dependents to accompany military personnel on their overseas tours.[25] During the Cold War, this practice was institutionalized and resulted in the construction of sprawling American military communities in Western Europe and Asia.

Strategic anchors, however, are evolving. The number of major combat units based abroad has shrunk considerably from Cold War peaks, and a return to such large deployments is unlikely, even with our closest allies. While some nations want to maintain legacy bases, few prospective allies desire or need a military presence on the scale of the Cold War. Four trends— population growth, the rise of nationalist sentiment (and the concomitant resentment toward the extraterritorial rights given to American forces), the increasingly free flow of information, and the expanding influence of public opinion on foreign policy—have made it more difficult for nations to host U.S. forces on their soil.

Forward Operating Locations

Second, although many FOLs are not constructed until a contingency occurs, when possible the United States works in peacetime with partner nations to identify and improve FOLs. FOLs are critical for ground forces and land-based air forces to generate and sustain operational effects during contingencies. USAF FOLs may be highly capable main operating bases or austere locations. For example, Aviano AB in Italy is a highly capable main operating base that could act as an FOL during North African contingencies. An example of an austere FOL would be Zamboanga International Airport on Mindanao Island in the Philippines. This FOL supports Joint Special Operations Task Force–Philippines.[26] In contrast to FOLs for air elements—which by definition are designed to create direct operational effects—ground force forward facilities serve a range of functions, from creating direct battlefield effects (primarily in counterinsurgency

---

[24] Pettyjohn, 2012, p. 99.

[25] Martha Gravois, "Military Families in Germany, 1946–1986: Why They Came and Why They Stayed," *Parameters, Journal of the US Army War College*, Vol. 16, No. 4, 1986, p. 58.

[26] Joint Special Operations Task Force–Philippines website, January 2013.

settings[27]) to providing depot or other support services. For our purposes, Army FOBs whose main activity is tactical operations in the immediate area are a particularly austere subset of FOLs. Larger Army FOBs and camps often serve both FOL and support link functions. Forward facilities for naval forces are generally focused on logistical support and in our framework are better viewed as support links (see below).

Many FOLs/FOBs are not constructed until an MCO occurs. For example, few of the dozens of facilities that U.S. forces operated from during the Korean War, the Vietnam War, in Iraq during OIF, or are currently operating from in Afghanistan existed as U.S. or partner nation bases prior to these interventions. In contrast, during Operation Desert Storm the USAF operated primarily from FOL airfields that had been developed for joint use with multiple Persian Gulf partners.

The USAF peacetime presence at contingency FOLs is generally minimal.[28] For example, there was no permanent operational USAF presence at air bases in Saudi Arabia, Bahrain, or Oman prior to Operation Desert Shield. In a major East Asia conflict, the USAF could conceivably operate from FOLs in many countries, yet in peacetime it has a significant presence at only six locations.[29] As noted above, FOL needs vary greatly, by service but the aviation elements of the four services all require some forward airfields to create operational effects. In this report, we'll focus on FOL airfields.

Support Links

Finally, the United States creates support links—ports, airfields, space tracking, and communication facilities—that act as connective tissue, allowing U.S. forces to move and communicate globally. USAF en route airfields are required to support both airlift and air refueling missions. For example, tanker aircraft operating from Moron AB in Spain provide air refueling support to USAF fighters transiting between the United States and forward bases in the Middle East. Naval air stations, such as NAS Sigonella in Italy, are also used as en route airfields by the USAF. (En route airfields will be discussed in more detail in Chapter Three.) Naval logistics support facilities, such as the U.S. Navy Region Singapore, provide critical support for fleet operations. Space tracking radars are located abroad at locations such as Thule Air Base, Greenland, providing "missile warning, space surveillance and space control."[30]

---

[27] During major conventional operations, ground maneuver elements generally create tactical effects through maneuver and typically do not use FOBs to support tactical operations (e.g., as firebases or sending out patrols).

[28] Due to the high threat from the Democratic People's Republic of Korea (DPRK) and potential for surprise attack, some USAF FOLs in South Korea (i.e., Osan and Kunsan ABs) are fully manned and operate as main operating bases and strategic anchors during peacetime.

[29] Osan and Kunsan ABs in Korea, Misawa, Yokota and Kadena ABs in Japan and Andersen AFB on Guam (U.S. territory).

[30] Description of 821st Air Base Group, Thule AB, Greenland mission from Peterson AFB website.

Communications facilities abroad (e.g., satellite downlinks) serve as part of DoD's global communications network.

An Integrated Framework for Posture Planning

These three activities and the requirements they are designed to meet comprise the posture triangle, illustrated in Figure 2.5. The posture triangle offers a logical framework that can integrate both qualitative and quantitative considerations. Every aspect of U.S. global posture can be explained in terms of the three triangle functions. The framework has utility for planners in the USAF, sister services, and DoD. Although DoD has implemented important posture innovations over the past decade, it has yet to present an integrated framework that answers the "why, what, where, and how" questions posed in Chapter One. It is hoped that the posture triangle will help DoD fill this gap.

Figure 2.5. The Posture Triangle

Forward Operating Locations

Conduct effective operations

U.S.

Strategic Anchors

Tie U.S. to closest allies

Sustain global Military activities

Support links

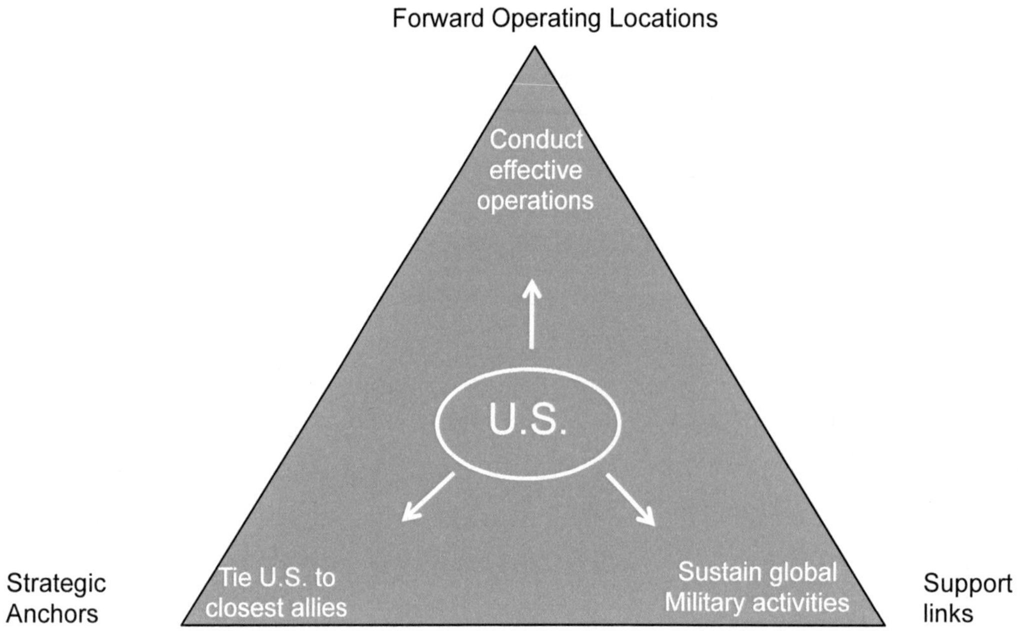

This chapter described the geographic advantages and limitations of U.S. territory for projecting military power abroad. It identified three requirements that can be met only through access to foreign soil. It also presented an analytical and planning framework—the posture triangle—to help analysts and planners link U.S. activities abroad to core national objectives.

The next chapter will apply the posture triangle to the question of where specifically the United States requires access overseas.

3. Where Does the USAF Need Basing and Access?

Current U.S. global posture is the product of both history and current demands. Many U.S. facilities have origins in conflicts dating back decades: to the 1990–1991 Gulf War, to the Korean War, and even to World War II. For example, Kadena AB in Japan originally (in 1945) supported U.S. occupation forces in the Ryuku Islands, then transitioned to support American and Japanese Cold War security needs. After the end of the Cold War, although the United States shed hundreds of facilities, it stayed at Kadena because the base continued (and continues) to serve a range of U.S. and Japanese defense activities. As we look to the future, however, the shifting geography and technological sophistication of emerging threats call for a reassessment of overseas base needs. Also, cost savings or efficiency arguments may, in peacetime, be particularly attractive but risk undermining the resiliency of the total basing network.[31] For these reasons, this chapter seeks to identify where the United States ought to have basing and access during both peacetime and contingencies. The answer is driven both by strategic considerations—which tend to be expressed qualitatively—and operational/tactical needs—which can generally be quantified. We return to the posture triangle to organize our discussion, beginning with strategic anchors.

Strategic Anchors

Strategic anchors can be viewed from a geographic or relational perspective. From the first perspective, one might argue that the United States needs close security partners in regions that both are vital and face significant military threats. In 2013, the greater Middle East and East Asia would be at the top of that list. Yet, strategic anchors also flow from relationships that predate current or emerging security challenges. These relationships produce benefits in the immediate region and support cooperative action farther afield.[32] For example, close relations between the

---

[31] The most authoritative contemporary treatment of global posture in general and posture costs in particular is Michael Lostumbo, Michael J. McNerney, Eric Peltz, Derek Eaton, David R. Frelinger, Victoria A. Greenfield, John Halliday, Patrick Mills, Bruce R. Nardulli, Stacie L. Pettyjohn, Jerry M. Sollinger, and Stephen Worman., *Overseas Basing of U.S. Military Forces: An Assessment of Relative Costs and Strategic Benefits*, Santa Monica, California. RAND Corporation, RR-201-OSD, 2013. Two other excellent analyses of the cost of USAF overseas bases are Jennifer Moroney, Patrick H. Mills, David T. Orletsky, and David E. Thaler, *Working with Allies and Partners: A Cost-Based Analysis of U.S. Air Forces in Europe,* Santa Monica, California: RAND Corporation, TR-1241-AF, 2012; and Patrick Mills, Adam Grissom, Jennifer Kavanagh, Leila Mahnad, and Stephen M. Worman., *The Costs of Commitment: Cost Analysis of Overseas Air Force Basing*, Santa Monica, Calif.: RAND Corporation, RR-150-AF, 2013.

[32] Whether basing forces in a partner nation causes greater cooperation is difficult to say. It is more likely that shared values and concern about threats (as will be discussed more in Chapter Four) leads to forward basing of U.S. forces, which then, in turn, offers greater opportunities for joint training, exercises, and security cooperation more broadly.

United States and its Western European security partners and years of security cooperation among NATO partners made possible effective concerted efforts to oppose Serbian ethnic cleansing in Kosovo during Operation Allied Force in 1999. Farther afield, European partners joined the United States in OIF and OEF. In addition to directly participating in combat operations in OEF, air mobility demands for those operations could not have been met without the support of strategic anchor countries such as the United Kingdom, Germany, Spain, and Italy. And the long history of security cooperation with European partners proved vital for effective joint action against Libya in Operation Odyssey Dawn in 2011. In 2013, French forces are taking the lead (with U.S. and other NATO support) in fighting an Islamic militant rebellion in Mali (including elements of Al Qaeda in the Islamic Maghreb). Over the coming years, U.S. and European partners are likely to increase security cooperation to prevent the creation of terrorist sanctuaries in North Africa. In short, the potential reach and broader national security benefit of strategic anchors is often greater than a narrow regional focus might suggest.

Strategic Anchors: Enduring Partners[33]

There are seven nations in the world that we identify as top-tier strategic anchors[34]—particularly close American security partners. All have hosted vital and permanent U.S. military facilities since the 1950s (or earlier) and have participated with the United States in recent military operations, including ongoing operations in Afghanistan. They are the United Kingdom, Germany, Italy, Spain, South Korea, Japan, and Australia[35] (See Figure 3.1).[36] An enduring military presence has been a key element of relations with these closest security partners for many decades.

---

[33] See Chapter Four for a more detailed discussion of the enduring partner concept.

[34] Our criteria for a top tier strategic anchor are (1) long-term hosting of key U.S. military facilities in central parts of the nation as opposed to noncontiguous territories, (2) close relations between U.S. and host nation militaries, and (3) host nation has participated with the United States in recent military operations.

[35] We recognize that no U.S. combat forces have been permanently based in Australia since World War II, but would argue that Australia is a top-tier strategic anchor because of the importance of the facilities that it has hosted, the number of times Australian forces have fought alongside U.S. forces, and the expanding access that Australia is giving U.S. forces, including hosting USMC rotational forces at Camp Robertson, near Darwin in the far north.

[36] The United States has had an enduring and valuable military presence in Turkey, Greece, and Portugal as well, but security cooperation with these nations has not been as deep or extensive as our top-tier nations.

Figure 3.1. U.S. Strategic Anchors in Europe, Southwest Asia, and East Asia

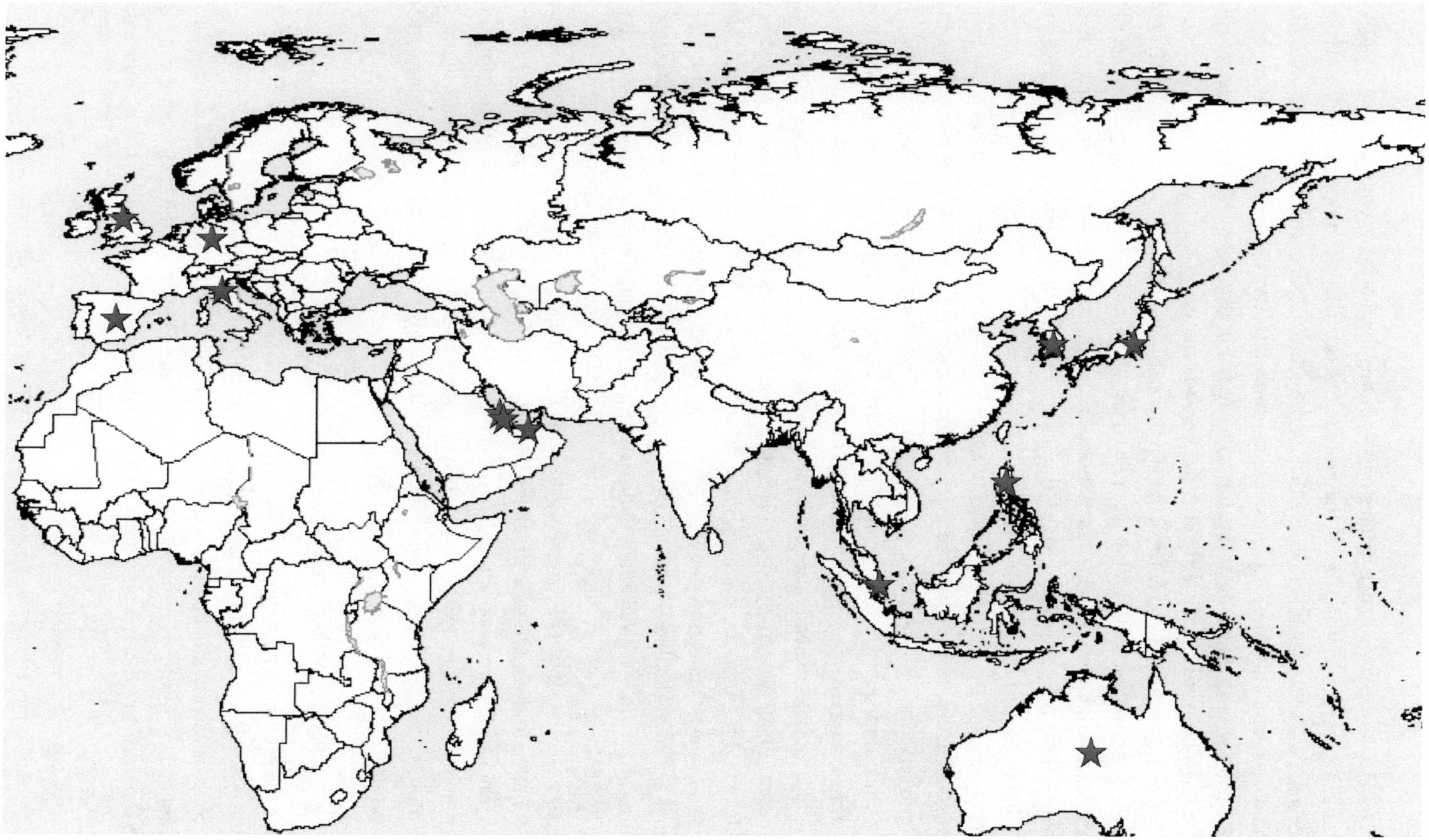

19

The U.S. military presence creates opportunities for routine exchanges, intelligence sharing, training, and exercises that provide the foundation for effective joint operations during contingencies. Although it is possible that close security cooperation could continue after the complete withdrawal of U.S. military forces from a country, experience to date suggests that the relationship will likely not be as deep or consistent. For example, U.S.-France security cooperation dropped significantly after the French ordered all U.S. forces out of the country in the 1960s, but it did not end entirely. This relationship has waxed and waned in the intervening years and is now much stronger due to joint operations in Libya, U.S. support to recent French operations in Mali, and, more broadly, mutual concerns about instability in North Africa. Although these are encouraging signs, the scale and depth of the cooperation does not compare with that of the top-tier anchors.

That said, a large Cold War–style presence is not necessary to realize these benefits. In some cases, a single military service can meet strategic anchor demands where today there may be multiple services. In some cases, consolidation of activities or reduction in forces may be appropriate. In the past, where forward forces have been reduced somewhat (for example, forward basing two rather than three squadrons in a fighter wing), an additional squadron has rotated forward periodically. For example, F-22 squadrons rotate on a regular basis to Kadena AB, Japan, to supplement the two F-15C squadrons permanently based there. Similar supplemental rotations are routinely done in Korea as well. Although relying exclusively on rotational forces is not an ideal alternative where a daily forward presence is required, they offer perhaps the most flexible and responsive force posture tool available to policymakers.

Increasingly, the United States will need to tailor its long-term presence to meet the specific security challenges and political constraints facing the host nation. This is nothing new. Indeed, the scope and nature of U.S. global posture has changed significantly over many decades and will continue to evolve to meet changing security demands. It may be smaller in the future, but a long-term military presence is likely to remain a key component of these relationships. Open, honest, and enduring cooperation and trust are the heart of the strategic anchor relationship; maintaining access to any particular facility should rarely be pursued at the expense of this partnership.[37]

Strategic Anchors—Mutual Defense Partners[38]

An enduring military presence has also proven valuable in regions where security relationships are not as advanced. In the Persian Gulf, Kuwait, Bahrain, Qatar, and the UAE have all shared U.S. concerns about potential regional threats and, as a result, have provided access for continuous U.S. military activities over many decades. That said, the size, scope, and visibility of these activities have been highly constrained by domestic political factors. Although important

---

[37] We thank reviewer Alexander Cooley for making this point.

[38] See Chapter Four for a more detailed discussion of the mutual defense partner concept.

partners and strategic anchors in their own right, these relationships do not have the depth and breadth that the United States enjoys with the top-tier anchor countries. These strategic anchors have supported a range of activities and deployments with considerable fluctuations during major contingencies, such as Operations Desert Storm, Enduring Freedom, and Iraqi Freedom.

For example, U.S. forces have been based or maintained prepositioned stocks and depots in Kuwait since 1991. The USN has been in Bahrain since 1948, when the U.S. Middle East Force was established. Naval Support Activity Bahrain has a permanent presence that includes 5th Fleet and Naval Forces Central Command headquarters.[39] USAF forces provide the principle presence in Qatar[40] and in the UAE,[41] but because of the political sensitivity of permanent garrisons, USAF forces deploy on a rotational rather than permanent basis to Al Udeid AB, Qatar, and Al Dhafra AB, UAE.

Providing presence via rotational forces is likely to become more common. For example, two current strategic anchors, Singapore and Australia, are both looking to expand the American military presence in their countries but do not want large permanent garrisons. Thus, the USN will be deploying the new littoral combat ship on 10-month rotations to Singapore,[42] and Australia will eventually host up to 2,500 U.S. marines on rotations through Camp Robertson near Darwin.[43] Finally, the Philippines, once a host to major U.S. bases and a host since 2002 to the U.S. Joint Special Operations Task Force–Philippines at Camp Navarro, Zamboanga (Mindanao),[44] may be reemerging as a strategic anchor. Philippine officials have stated publicly that the country will host both USN[45] and USAF[46] rotational forces at Subic Bay in the near

---

[39] CNIC Naval Support Activity Bahrain website, "NSA Bahrain History."

[40] Christopher M. Blanchard, *Qatar: Background and U.S. Relations,* Washington, D.C.: Congressional Research Service, 2012, p. 12. The National Defense Authorization Act for Fiscal Year 2008 authorized $22.3 million for construction in support of USAF operations at Al Udeid AB. See Public Law 110-181 (January 28, 2008), Sec. 2301, Authorized Air Force Construction and Land Acquisition Projects, Washington, D.C.: U.S. Congress, p. 514. For more on the U.S. military presence in the Persian Gulf, see U.S. Senate, *The Gulf Security Architecture: Partnership with the Gulf Cooperation Council,* a majority staff report prepared for the use of the Committee on Foreign Relations, United States Senate, One Hundred Twelfth Congress, Second Session, Washington, D.C.: U.S. Government Printing Office, June 19, 2012, pp. 9–19.

[41] See U.S. House of Representatives, *Making Emergency Supplemental Appropriations for the Fiscal Year Ending September 30, 2005, and for Other Purposes,* Conference Report 109-72, Washington, D.C., 2005, pp. 121–122.

[42] Jim Wolf, "U.S. Plans 10-month Warship Deployment to Singapore," *Reuters Online,* May 10, 2012.

[43] Matt Siegel, "As Part of Pact, U.S. Marines Arrive in Australia, in China's Strategic Backyard," *The New York Times,* April 4, 2012.

[44] The U.S. Joint Special Operations Task Force–Philippines website describes the mission as follows: "At the request of the Philippine Government, JSOTF-P works together with the Armed Forces of the Philippines to fight terrorism and deliver humanitarian assistance to the people of Mindanao. U.S. forces are temporarily deployed to the Philippines in a strictly non-combat role to advise and assist the AFP, share information, and to conduct joint civil military operations."

[45] Michael Cohen and James Hardy, "Philippines, U.S. Confirm U.S. Navy's Return to Subic Bay," *Jane's Online,* October 12, 2012.

[46] Carlo Munoz, "The Philippines Re-Opens Military Bases to U.S. Forces," *DEFCON Hill,* June 6, 2012.

future. U.S. officials are more cautious and will only acknowledge that discussions are taking place between the two governments about this possibility.[47]

So far, the only access-related step forward announced by the U.S. government was the Philippine government decision to streamline "the diplomatic clearance process for U.S. military aircraft and ships, enhancing opportunities for training and interoperability."[48]

Forward Operating Locations

Strategic anchor locations sometimes act as FOLs, but strategic anchors are too few in number and too geographically concentrated to meet potential U.S. demands across a wide range of contingencies. FOL characteristics vary by scenario and specific mission, but for most platforms they need to be within 1500nm of the operating area to avoid excessive force structure demands. Runway length and strength, parking ramp size, and fuel storage capacity are the other primary considerations. The USAF need not maintain a presence or have routine peacetime access to contingency FOLs. Indeed, during major contingencies the USAF regularly operates out of FOLs where it has neither.[49] Figure 3.2 displays airfields used by the USAF in five major combat operations. In every case, the USAF operated out of at least a few airfields where it had no prior peacetime access, and in three conflicts (Vietnam, Operation Desert Storm, and Operation Allied Force) the new airfields outnumbered those where the USAF had prior access.

---

[47] Dempsey, Martin E., "Gen. Dempsey Briefs the Pentagon Press Corps," June 7, 2012.

[48] U.S. Department of State, "Toward a Deeper Alliance: United States–Philippines Bilateral Cooperation," fact sheet, January 27, 2012.

[49] For example, the United States had no access to Bagram Air Field prior to OEF nor to Balad Air Base prior to OIF.

Figure 3.2. Airfields Used by the USAF During Five Major Combat Operations

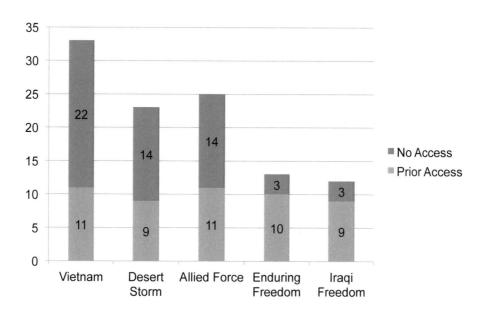

NOTE: Bases in Vietnam were considered "prior access" if the USAF had access to them prior to the Gulf of Tonkin Incident in 1964.

Although the historical experience suggests the USAF will need to maintain a capability to rapidly develop airfields during conflicts, the preferred approach would be to work with security partners to identify and improve potential FOLs during peacetime.

To better understand where the USAF needs FOLs, over the past two years RAND assessed the operational demands associated with 28 scenarios.[50] As Figure 3.3 illustrates, the scenarios were geographically diverse, with locations in the South Pacific, South America, European Arctic, Africa, Middle East, Southwest Asia, Indian Ocean, Southeast Asia, and Northeast Asia.

---

[50] For more details on these scenarios, see Vick and Heim, *Assessing U.S. Air Force Basing Options in East Asia*, Santa Monica, Calif.: RAND Corporation, MG-1204-AF, 2013, not available to the general public; and Jeff Hagen and Jacob L. Heim, *USAF Global Posture: Using Scenario Analysis to Identify Future Basing and Force Requirements* Santa Monica, Calif.: RAND Corporation, RR-405-AF, forthcoming.

Figure 3.3. Analytic Scenario Locations

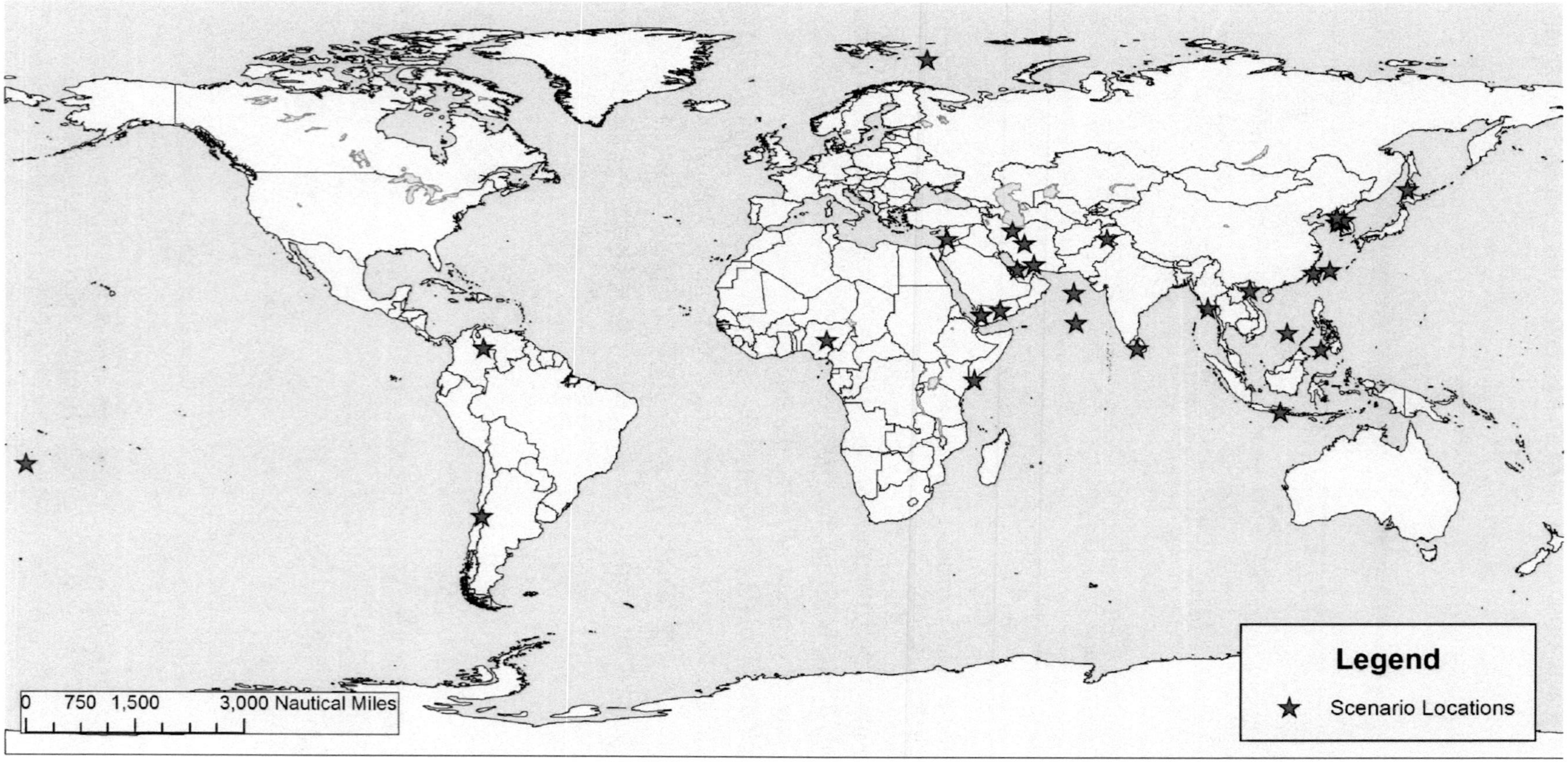

Legend

Scenario Locations

★ Scenario Locations

750 1,500   3,000 Nautical Miles

24

The study scenarios were also diverse in mission demands, covering six major contingency types:

- Natural disaster
- Civil conflict
- Insurgency/terrorism/piracy
- Limited conflict/crisis
- MCOs
- Nuclear proliferation or threats of nuclear use.

Table 3.1 displays scenarios by contingency type. Note that there are at least two scenarios for every category and that there is geographic diversity within every category. Most scenarios fell into the insurgency/terrorism/piracy or limited conflict/crisis categories, but we also explored four MCOs: two involving China; a war between the Democratic People's Republic of Korea (DPRK) and the Republic of Korea (ROK); and a conflict with Iran. Representative missions for these contingencies included airlift; enduring intelligence, surveillance, and reconnaissance (ISR); air superiority; long-range strike; interdiction; and missile defense.

Table 3.1. Scenarios Used to Identify FOL Demands

Scenario Location	Natural Disaster	Civil Conflict	insurgency/Terrorism/ Piracy	Limited conflict/Crisis	MCO	Nuclear proliferation or threat
Sri Lanka	X					
Tonga	X					
Chile	X					
Burma		X				
Syria		X				
Yemen			X			
Indonesia			X			
Philippines			X			
Yemen			X			
Nigeria			X			
Kenya/Somalia			X			
Northern Arabian Sea			X			
Spratly Islands				X		
Senkaku Islands				X		
Yeonpyeong Island				X		
Kuril Islands				X		
Persian Gulf				X		
Iran				X		
Svaalbard Island				X		
Colombia-Venezuela border				X		
Yemen				X		
Pakistan				X		
China/Vietnam					X	
China/Taiwan					X	
DPRK-ROK					X	
Iran					X	
DPRK						X
Indian Ocean						X

This study assessed the relative utility of airfields as potential FOLs on several dimensions, including airfield capacity and distance to scenario. Using a representative mission, we measured force structure demands for alternative airfields and scored them based on whether they were light, moderate, or heavy.[51] A key finding from this research was that there is no shortage of potential FOLs. For example, as shown in Figure 3.4, in the vicinity of the South China Sea there are more than 100 airfields[52] capable of supporting F-16 operations. Although an MCO scenario in this region might call for one to two dozen airfields, most scenarios that we assessed required only a handful of airfields. This gives the United States flexibility in choosing locations and also resilience in the face of access denial or changes in threats. A portfolio of airfields with a few locations in multiple Southeast Asian countries would offer a robust posture.

---

[51] For details of the overall scenario and force structure analysis, see Hagen and Heim, forthcoming. For additional details on East Asia scenario analysis see Vick and Heim, 2013.

[52] 101 airfields are displayed. Forty-nine of these can support fighter aircraft (F-16) only; another 52 can support both F-16s and C-17 aircraft. The F-16 capable runways were determined using two factors: minimum of 7,500 feet in length and an ACN/PCN (Aircraft Classification Number/Pavement Classification Number) ratio of 1.0 or less. Airfield technical information was derived from the Automated Air Facility Information File (AAFIF), ACN data from USAF engineering documents and reports. Thanks to Steve Worman for this analysis.

Figure 3.4. F-16 Capable Airfields in Southeast Asia

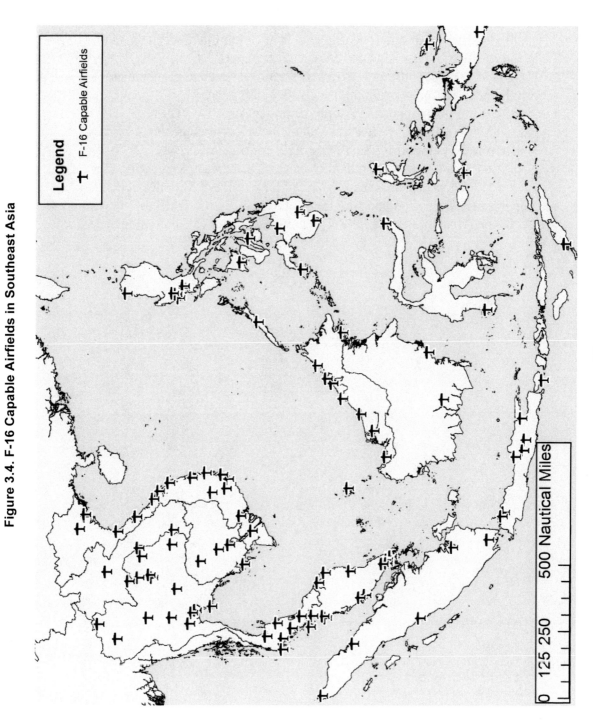

27

This analysis found that when scored across multiple scenarios and operational dimensions, airfields across a relatively large area performed similarly. We call these groups "basing clusters"[53] and recommend that the USAF seek to develop a portfolio of airfields across nations in each cluster. Figure 3.5 displays 11 clusters that were identified during the scenario analysis:

1. South America (supporting contingencies in Colombia/Venezuela and Chile)
2. Western Africa (supporting contingencies in Nigeria[54])
3. Horn of Africa (supporting Kenya and Southwest Asia contingencies)
4. Southern/Eastern Europe (supporting Iran contingencies)
5. Northern Europe (supporting Arctic contingency)
6. Persian Gulf (supporting Iran and Indian Ocean contingencies)
7. Western India (supporting Southwest Asia contingencies)
8. Southeast Asia (supporting Indian Ocean and Southeast Asia contingencies)
9. Australia (supporting Southeast Asia and East Asia MCO contingencies)
10. Yap/Palau/Marianas (supporting East Asia MCO contingencies)
11. Northeast Asia (supporting DPRK, Japan-Russia and MCO contingencies).

---

[53] The basing cluster idea was first developed by David Frelinger and team for the Project AIR FORCE FY11 Southwest Asia basing study. We found the idea applied more generally and used it in both the FY11 East Asia and FY 12 global posture studies.

[54] Although we did not assess a counterinsurgency/counterterror scenario in Mali, the airfields (e.g., Diori Hamani in western Niger) that we identified in this cluster are well located for operations over Mali.

Figure 3.5. Global Basing Clusters

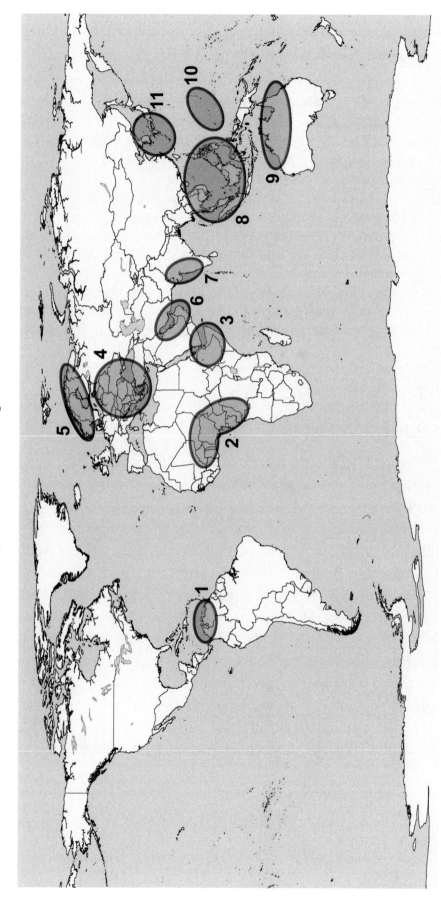

NOTE: See Hagen and Heim (forthcoming) for more details on basing clusters.

Expanded access in these clusters is necessary for effective operations in the scenarios we assessed. A few key insights from this analysis include:

- Airfields in the Southern/Eastern Europe cluster are useful for MCOs in Southwest Asia. Airfields in this area are outside of the worst missile threat rings but also within range for fighter operations.[55]
- Airfields in the western Africa cluster (e.g., Diori Hamani in Niger) can support ISR operations over much of Northwest Africa and are well positioned to conduct counterterror or counterinsurgency operations in Mali, Nigeria, Algeria, Libya, and Chad.
- Airfields in the Horn of Africa cluster can support ISR operations over much of Northeast Africa as well as fighter and ISR operations on the Arabian Peninsula.
- Airfields in the Southeast Asia cluster are necessary to sustain operations in the South China Sea crisis scenarios and in a Vietnam/China conflict, but would be within the worst missile threat rings in a major war.
- Airfields in the Australian cluster are outside of the worst missile threat rings and could provide needed strategic depth and sanctuary in major conflict scenarios.
- Airfields in the Yap/Palau/Marianas cluster are essential dispersal bases for major conflicts in East Asia.
- Locations in the Eastern/Southern Europe, Horn of Africa, and Southeast Asia basing clusters are most versatile across the 28 scenarios.

Support Links (En Route Airfields)

As noted in Chapter Two, support links include global networks of communication facilities, ports, and airfields. In this analysis we assessed the utility of a key support link element—the USAF air mobility network.

The USAF maintains a global network of "en route" airfields to support air mobility activities. These airfields are positioned to (1) provide redundant routes for airlift aircraft across the Atlantic and Pacific Oceans and (2) support air refueling "tracks" (e.g., to support fighter aircraft deployments). To provide redundancy in the event of poor weather or political access problems as well as the most direct routes to various destinations, the USAF maintains two routes across the Pacific and three across the Atlantic. The cross-ocean routes are (1) northern Pacific route (Alaska to Japan), (2) southern Pacific route (Hawaii to Guam to Japan or Southeast Asia), (3) northern Atlantic route (Delaware to United Kingdom or Germany), (4) mid-Atlantic route (Delaware to Spain), and (5) southern Atlantic route (Delaware to Caribbean to Ascension Island to Africa). These en route locations are not all USAF bases. Some are USN or USMC bases, some are military facilities of partner nations (e.g., Ascension Island), and others are commercial airfields.

They vary from highly capable major bases (e.g., Ramstein AB, Germany) to facilities with little or no daily USAF presence (e.g., V.C. Bird International Airport, Antigua). Air Mobility

---

[55] David Frelinger et al., "Assessing Options for Future USAF Force Posture in SWA," unpublished RAND briefing, August 2011.

Command categorizes these locations into four tiers based on capacity and manning. There are only three Tier I facilities in the world: Ramstein AB, Germany; Naval Station Rota, Spain; and Joint Base Pearl Harbor-Hickam, Hawaii. Figure 3.6 shows the locations and tier level for the current en route network.

To gain insight into future demands for en route airfields, we assessed the utility of the current network across the 28 scenarios discussed earlier. Our assessment method scored airfields based on their distance to representative FOLs[56] in 12 regions. All scenario FOLs are within these regions. Table 3.2 displays the results of the assessment. Airfields are scored green if less than or equal to 2,000nm distance to a FOL, yellow if 2,000–3,500nm, and red if greater than 3,500nm.[57] We assigned versatility scores to airfields based on the number of yellow and green scores they received. The names of the highest-scoring airfields are shown in blue type.[58] As might be expected, airfields in Europe and the Middle East were most versatile given their proximity to the African, Southwest Asia, and European FOLs. Airfields in Southeast Asia, Japan, and Australia scored high for some East Asian regions but were generally less versatile. Airfields in Hawaii, Alaska, and Latin America/Caribbean were the least versatile.

Table 3.3 displays the 35 en route airfields that the RAND assessment identified as most valuable. They were either among the 15 highest-scoring on the versatility index, critical for a priority scenario, part of a cross-ocean route, or destination airfields in Afghanistan.

---

[56] Representative FOLs are Rio de Janeiro, Brazil; Diori Haman, Niger; Laikipia, Kenya; Camp Lemonier, Djibouti; Al Udeid, Qatar; Bagram, Afghanistan; Mihail Kogainiceanu, Romania; Bodo, Norway; Changi West, Singapore; Royal Australian Air Force Base Darwin, Australia; Osan AB, Korea; and Auckland, New Zealand.

[57] AMC uses 2,000nm as the planning factor unrefueled operating radius for the C-17 (outbound with load, engines running offload, and return empty). AMC uses 3,500nm as the planning factor for a fully loaded one-way trip. These are conservative numbers. Extended range C-17s have much greater range at 4,400nm one-way with 45 short-ton load. See AMC (2010).

[58] This should not be interpreted to mean that airfields scoring sevens are superior facilities; the score is simple a measure of proximity to scenarios. For example, Moron AB in Spain scored 7 while Rota NAS in Spain scored 6. The two airfields are less than 50 miles apart, and Rota is a more capable airfield, ranked by AMC as a Tier I location, in contrast to Moron, which is a Tier III.

Figure 3.6. Air Mobility Command En Route Airfields

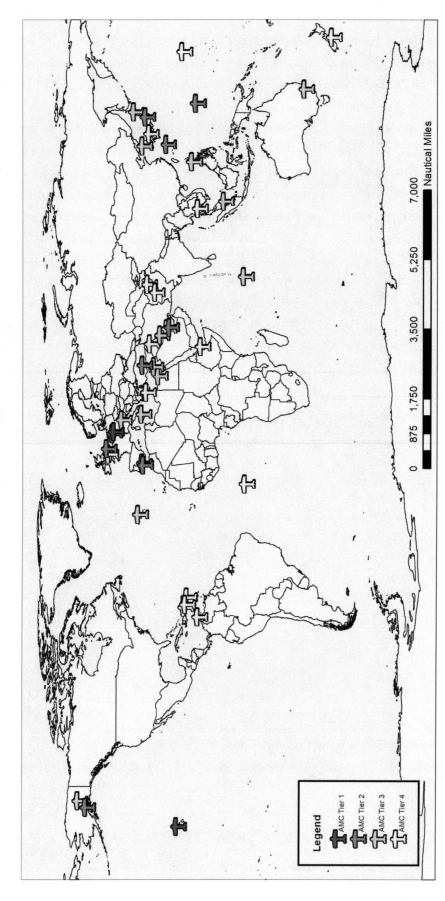

SOURCE: RAND map based on data from AMC (2010).

32

Table 3.2. Performance of En Route Locations Across Scenario Locations

Airfield/Scenario locations	South America	West Africa	East Africa	Horn of Africa	Persian Gulf	Central Asia	East Europe	N Europe	SEA	N AUS	NEA	AUS/NZ	Versatility #G & Y Scores
Antigua													1
Palanguero, Colombia													1
Mildenhall													6
Spangdahlem													7
Ramstein													7
Aviano													7
Incirlik													7
Souda Bay													7
Sigonella													7
Mihail Kogalniceanu, Romania							FOL						6
Lajes													4
Moron													7
Rota													6
Cairo West													7
Al Udeid					FOL								7
Al Mubarak													7
Djibouti				FOL									6
Ascension													2
Diego Garcia													6
Singapore									FOL				4
U-Tapao													6
Subic Bay													4
Richmond													3
Elmendorf													1
Hickam													0
Wake													3
Andersen													4
Osan											FOL		3
Kadena													4
Yokota													4

33

Table 3.3. Most Valuable En Route Locations

Airfield/Scoring Criteria	Tier	Versatility	Critical scenario	Cross-Ocean En Route Location	OEF
Antigua	IV			X	
Ascencion	IV			X	
Mildenhall	III	X		X	
Fairford	IV	X		X	
Spangdahlem	II	X		X	
Ramstein	I	X		X	
Aviano	III	X			
Incirlik	II	X			
Souda Bay	II	X			
Sigonella	IV	X			
Mihail Kogalniceanu	IV	X			
Moron	III	X		X	
Rota	I	X		X	
Al Mubarek	III	X			
Bahrain	IV	X			
Al Udeid	II	X			
Djibouti	III	X			
Bagram	III				X
Kandahar	IV				X
Diego Garcia	III	X			
U-Tapao	III	X			
Elemendorf	II		X	X	
Eilson	III			X	
JBPearl-Hickam	I		X	X	
Wake	IV		X		
Andersen	II		X	X	
Saipan	IV		X	X	
Subic Bay	IV		X	X	
Singapore	IV		X	X	
Cam Ranh Bay	IV		X	X	
Richmond	IV			X	
Misawa	III			X	
Yokota	II		X	X	
Kadena	II		X	X	
Osan	III		X		

NOTE: Although it scored well on the versatility metric, we did not include Cairo West (a Tier IV airfield) in this list. Given the current instability in Egypt and great uncertainty about future U.S. use of this location, we recommend against its inclusion in the en route plan. The United States has many good alternatives to Cairo West in the Mediterranean, Horn of Africa, and Persian Gulf.

Note that some regions have multiple en route airfields in relatively close proximity (e.g., Ramstein and Spangdahlem, Rota and Moron) and that in some cases there are more airfields than needed if C-17 range were the only consideration (e.g., Sigonella, Souda Bay and Incirlik in the Mediterranean littoral). Although some streamlining of en route locations may be possible, much of what appears at first blush to be redundant is driven by the capacity needed to support major operations. That is, there is not sufficient capacity at a single location (e.g., Ramstein AB) to meet en route needs during major contingencies. Also, multiple locations provide redundancy in the event of weather problems, political access constraints, or adversary threats to airfields.

We did not analyze airfield capacity in this study, but would offer a more general observation about en route structure. Given the small investment required to sustain AMC activities at most airfields and their enormous value during contingencies, we suggest that network resiliency considerations should drive en route investment decisions rather than peacetime cost saving or efficiency arguments.

In this chapter, we identified those locations where the United States ought to maintain or develop strategic anchors, FOLs, and en route airfields. We also described our approach to scenario analysis, using dozens of geographically and mission diverse contingencies to access U.S. global posture needs. Having considered where the USAF needs access to meet both operational and strategic goals, we now move to the difficult question of political access. Reliability of access varies greatly across nations and represents a key uncertainty and risk for policymakers. The next chapter seeks to identify the factors associated with access risk and thereby to help inform choices regarding where the United States should seek peacetime access and basing.

4. What Types of Security Partnerships Minimize Peacetime Access Risk?

In September 2009, U.S. forces were expelled from Manta AB in Ecuador after President Rafael Correra refused to renew the lease because "sovereignty is not having foreign soldiers on the fatherland's soil."[59] Consequently, the United States found itself searching for an air base that its surveillance aircraft could use to monitor and interdict drug trafficking in Latin America for the second time in a decade.[60] Despite the relatively small U.S. military presence at Manta (which typically consisted of approximately 250 military personnel), the United States had to make more than $70 million in improvements so that the airfield could support E-3 Sentry aircraft.[61] Although the USAF presence at Manta helped to stem the flow of illegal drugs from South America, Correra felt that the base provided few benefits to his nation and risked entangling Ecuador in a conflict with Colombia.[62] For these reasons, he insisted that American forces leave the base when the lease expired in 2009.[63]

The U.S. experience at Manta raises an important question: Where is basing risky and where is it reliable? In other words, where are U.S. forces at risk of being expelled or having their peacetime basing rights limited? Conversely, which nations are likely to provide stable peacetime access for the foreseeable future?[64] This chapter seeks to answer these questions by exploring the effect that security partnerships and host nation regime type have on peacetime access.

---

[59] Quoted in Mike Cesar, "Rising Nationalism Threatens U.S. Anti-Drug Base in Ecuador," *World Politics Review*, April 30, 2008.

[60] The United States had been unable to extend its access to Howard Air Force Base in Panama in 1999. Larry Rohter, "U.S. Accord With Panama on troops Hits a Snag," *New York Times*, April 26, 1998; Christopher Sandars, *America's Overseas Garrisons: The Leasehold Empire*, Oxford: Oxford University Press, 2000, pp. 139–140.

[61] Other FOLs in Latin America include El Salvador, Aruba, and Curacao; see U.S. General Accounting Office, *Drug Control: International Counterdrug Sites Being Developed*, December 2000; Samuel Logan, "U.S. Faces Eviction from Ecuadorian Base," *ISN Security Watch*, January 12, 2007.

[62] The USAF flew 100 counternarcotics flights from Manta, and by 2009 these operations had reportedly contributed to the seizure of 1,800 metric tons of illegal drugs worth $36 billion. Simon Romero, "Ecuador's Leader Purges Military and Moves to Expel American Base," *New York Times*, April 21, 2008; and GlobalSecurity.org, "Eloy Alfaro Air Base/FOL Manta, Ecuador."

[63] Andrew Yeo, *Activists, Alliances, and Anti-U.S. Base Protests*, Cambridge: Cambridge University Press, 2011, pp. 87–100.

[64] These questions are focused on challenges to the United States' peacetime access to bases in foreign countries, which is distinct from contingency access. The former are locations where the United States has steady-state rights to use military facilities in another country, while the latter is the permission to use a facility or the forces stationed at a foreign base for a particular operation.

The focus on peacetime access risk is warranted for a number of reasons. First, as mentioned in the discussion of strategic anchors in Chapter Two, an important reason that the United States stations forces overseas is to visibly bind it to the host nation and the broader region. Forward-based U.S. forces help to promote stability by deterring potential adversaries, reassuring allies, and countering persistent threats to the commons, which are peacetime missions. Thus, while access to foreign bases during a contingency is critical, it is equally important to identify which nations provide stable access for steady-state missions.

Second, the United States is in the midst of rebalancing its defense posture away from the regions where it has traditionally maintained a large overseas presence (i.e., Western Europe) toward Asia. As the United States implements this shift, it is essential that DoD distinguish between nations that are likely to provide stable peacetime access and those that are more likely to circumscribe or rescind U.S. basing rights. This is especially important in the context of shrinking defense budgets. DoD does not want to waste its scarce resources building new bases or improving existing facilities only to lose access to these locations. Given the investments and the time that it takes to build or improve overseas facilities so that they can support U.S. military operations, the United States should prioritize countries that are likely to provide stable peacetime access. This is particularly important for strategic anchors; that is, those locations where the U.S. plans to permanently station forces overseas.

Third, basing issues often dominate the United States' relationship with a host nation and can distract security partners from more important issues or undermine an otherwise strong bilateral relationship.[65] Fourth, contentious base politics can damage the United States' international reputation and its credibility, particularly if a host nation evicts U.S. forces. Consequently, potential adversaries as well as allies may question the ability of the United States to maintain its military presence in a region and uphold its security commitments.

Political Challenges to Peacetime Access

The international environment is changing in ways that could make it more difficult for the United States to secure and maintain access to bases abroad. Originally, overseas bases were largely a product of colonialism, as imperial powers established military outposts in their dependencies.[66] Although some critics argue that the U.S. overseas military presence is a modern form of imperialism, these claims ignore the fact that in the post–World War II era the United States has generally stationed its forces in countries that have voluntarily agreed to host them,

---

[65] Alexander Cooley, *Base Politics: Democratic Change and The U.S. Military Overseas*, Ithaca, N.Y.: Cornell University Press, 2008, p. 4; Alexander Cooley and Hendrik Spruyt, *Contracting States: Sovereign Transfers in International* Relations, Princeton, N.J.: Princeton University Press, 2009, p. 101.

[66] Robert E. Harkavy, *Bases Abroad: The Global Foreign Military Presence*, New York: Oxford University Press, 1989, pp. 3, 23.

creating an "empire by invitation."[67] In fact, DoD acquired rights to many of the foreign bases that it still has today during the early years of the Cold War, when other nations were particularly willing to grant the United States base access. Not only was the United States the dominant global power, but nearly all of its allies had been devastated by World War II, leaving them unable to provide for their own security.[68] In addition to this large power disparity, after the outbreak of the Korean War noncommunist nations saw the Soviet Union as an unambiguous threat, which made them more amenable to hosting U.S. forces. Furthermore, the United States did not have to contend with public opposition to its overseas military presence, since most of these host nations were led by autocratic governments that ignored public opinion or because host nation elites and the general public both supported the U.S. military presence.[69] Due to this convergence of factors, basing agreements reached in the late 1940s and early 1950s usually provided the United States exclusive rights to large facilities and offered U.S. personnel extensive extraterritorial privileges. Consequently, the United States constructed sprawling main operating bases, or "Little Americas," that housed U.S. military personnel and their families.[70]

Despite the threat posed by the Soviet Union and other communist nations, gaining and maintaining access to overseas facilities became increasingly difficult as the Cold War progressed, due in large part to two closely related trends: the strengthening norm of sovereignty and the increasing influence of public opinion. The growing importance of nationalism and popular sensitivity regarding sovereignty generated public opposition to a U.S. military presence, and the spread of democracy compelled host nation governments to take public opinion into account. Moreover, these challenges have arguably become even greater in the post–Cold War era due to the proliferation of information and communications technologies, which have helped to publicize America's global military presence and mobilize local, national, and transnational opposition networks.

First, as the norm of sovereignty has become increasingly rooted in the international system, there has been a concomitant rise in nationalism, yielding a greater unwillingness to tolerate a

---

[67] This term was coined by Geir Lundestad, "Empire by Invitation? The United States and Western Europe, 1945–1952," *Journal of Peace Research*, Vol. 23, No. 3, September 1986, pp. 263–277. Cooley and Spruyt characterize U.S. basing agreements as incomplete contracts in which the host nation retains residual sovereign rights, but the United States obtains rights of access. Cooley and Spruyt, 2009, pp. 101–102. Exceptions to the norm of voluntary hosts include Okinawa prior to its reversion to Japanese sovereignty in 1972, the Panama Canal Zone, Guantanamo Bay, Cuba, and occupations in the aftermath of wars. Sandars, 2000, pp. 126–138, 161–166.

[68] For more on the history of the U.S. global defense posture, see Pettyjohn, 2012.

[69] Anni P. Baker, *American Soldiers Overseas: The Global Military Presence*, Westport, Conn.: Praeger, 2004, p. 48.

[70] In the postwar era, main operating bases were seen reducing tensions by eliminating the need for U.S. personnel to requisition local housing and separating the relatively wealthy Americans from the impoverished local population. This is not to suggest that the relationship was without problems, but rather that in general there was elite and public support for the U.S. military presence, especially in Europe. Baker, 2004, pp. 43–48, 53–58. See also Mark L. Gillem, *America Town: Building the Outposts of Empire*, Minneapolis: University of Minnesota Press, 2007.

foreign military presence.[71] In its ideal form, sovereignty means that "no higher juridical authority exists above that of the national government," which implies that external actors are excluded from the state.[72] Because this uncompromised notion of sovereignty rarely exists, there is tension between a public's desire for this absolute principle and a government's willingness to compromise these rights by permitting foreign forces on its soil.[73] Moreover, since powerful states are usually the ones that establish bases in weaker nations, the public often sees these facilities as a form of imperial domination, especially if they are located in a former colony or a nation that has been forcibly occupied.[74] For these reasons, negotiations over the sovereign status of a base itself (whether it is an exclusively American base, a host nation base where American forces are tenants, or a shared/joint facility) are often extremely controversial.

Status of forces agreements (SOFAs)—the treaties that delineate who has jurisdiction over U.S. military personnel—are another point of contention related to sovereignty.[75] The issue of criminal jurisdiction often becomes a flashpoint that leads to widespread protests if a U.S. serviceperson commits a high-profile crime but is not tried by the host nation's judicial system, especially if the accused is ultimately acquitted or receives what the local community regards to be a light sentence. In short, the general public often sees U.S. bases as a form of subordination or an insult to national pride, while the host government is more likely to accept a U.S. military presence because of the security or the material benefits that it provides. Because of this sensitivity, host nations often compare the terms of their SOFA with other countries to determine their standing vis-à-vis the United States and the international community more broadly.

The sentiment that a nation should be the supreme authority in its land has grown over time and become "an ever more entrenched principle of the international system."[76] In the post–World War II era, the process of decolonization presented an early challenge to U.S. basing rights. In the late 1940s, the administration of President Harry Truman decided to side with the European empires against colonies that were pursuing self-determination because doing so was believed to

---

[71] Nationalism maintains that a nation—which has a distinctive culture and history—should have its own political state. Nationalist sentiment is anger at violations of this principle. Ernest Gellner and John Breuilly, *Nations and Nationalism*, second edition, Ithaca, N.Y.: Cornell University Press, 2009, pp. 1–2.

[72] Cooley and Spruyt, 2009, p. 1; this definition of sovereignty is similar to what Stephen Krasner calls Westphalian sovereignty. See Stephen D. Krasner, *Sovereignty: Organized Hypocrisy*, Princeton: Princeton University Press, 1999, p. 4.

[73] Joseph Gerson, "The Sun Never Sets," in Joseph Gerson and Bruce Birchard, eds., *The Sun Never Sets: Confronting the Network of Foreign U.S. Military Bases*, Boston, Mass.: South End Press, 1991, p. 14. For more on sovereignty being compromised see Cooley and Spruyt, 2009, or Krasner, 1999, p. 24.

[74] Catherin Lutz, "Introduction: Bases, Empire, and Global Response," in Catherine Lutz, ed., *The Bases of Empire: The Global Struggle Against U.S. Military Posts*, New York: New York University Press, 2009, p. 30. See also Gerson, 1991, pp. 14–17; and Kent E. Calder, *Embattled Garrisons: Comparative Base Politics and American Globalism*, Princeton, N.J.: Princeton University Press, 2007, pp. 232–233.

[75] For more on SOFAs, see R. Chuck Mason, *Status of Forces Agreement (SOFA): What Is It, and How Has It Been Utilized?* Washington, D.C.: Congressional Research Service, March 15, 2012.

[76] Cooley and Spruyt, 2009, p. 15.

advance U.S. interests. In the short term, this decision did indeed help the United States to contain the Soviet Union, as Great Britain and France provided the United State with rights to important air bases in their North African colonies of Libya and Morocco.[77] However, by the mid-1950s many former dependencies had secured their independence, and local populations saw U.S. garrisons as a new form of empire. Despite this, the rulers of Libya and Morocco initially permitted the bases to remain because they provided their governments with valuable revenue. Eventually, however, nationalist resentment toward these bases reached a crescendo, compelling Libya and Morocco to severely restrict and eventually rescind U.S. access.[78]

Nationalism remains an issue today that discourages governments from hosting U.S. forces and limits the type of basing rights that they are willing to provide. For example, even some close allies that regularly host rotationally deployed U.S. forces still refuse to allow permanent foreign military bases on their territory. The government of Australia, for one, has resolutely opposed the notion that the USMC presence at Camp Robertson is a U.S. base. Instead, the Australian government has emphasized the temporary and joint nature of the U.S. presence.[79]

The second trend is the expanding influence of public opinion on basing decisions, largely due to the diffusion of democracy. The movement toward more participatory and contested forms of government has been uneven, with periods of democratization often occurring in unanticipated "waves" that are followed by periods of backsliding.[80] Nevertheless, the expansion of democracy is undeniable.[81] As will be discussed in more detail later, over the long term the spread of democracy could produce more stable access agreements, but in the short term it almost inevitably leads to greater restrictions on U.S. basing rights. In democratic regimes, institutions such as regular elections and legislative ratification allow citizens to directly hold their leaders accountable for the policies that they implement. As a result, democratic leaders cannot easily ignore local opposition to U.S. bases. In the Philippines, for example, the constitution stipulates that the senate must approve the deployment of any foreign forces to the

---

[77] Melvyn P. Leffler, *A Preponderance of Power: National Security, the Truman Administration, and the Cold War*, Stanford, Calif.: Stanford University Press, 1993, pp. 226–227.

[78] Sandars, 2000, pp. 48–50; Baker, 2004, pp. 51–52, 70–72.

[79] According to Defence Minister Stephen Smith, "We don't have United States military bases in Australia and we are not proposing to. What we have talked about in terms of either increased aerial access or naval access is precisely that—greater access to our facilities." Naomi Woodley, "Smith: No US bases in Australia," *ABC News*, August 2, 2012. Smith maintained "the US does not have permanent military bases on Australian territory and this will not change. The activities will take place in Australian facilities." Stephen Smith, "Remarks to the Australian Strategic Policy Institute (ASPI), Australia's Changing Circumstances," August 1, 2012.

[80] Samuel P. Huntington, *The Third Wave: Democratization in the Late Twentieth Century*, Norman, Okla.: University of Oklahoma Press, 1991, pp. 13–26.

[81] For example, Freedom House identifies 46 nations that have become "free" since 1972, which is an increase of 17 percent. Arch Puddington, *Freedom in the World 2013: Democratic Breakthroughs in the Balance*, 2013.

islands.[82] Increasingly, a host government and the United States must take steps to defuse anti-base sentiment, which frequently emerges in the communities located near U.S. bases. These communities suffer the most from the various negative externalities—including environmental degradation, noise pollution, and safety hazards—associated with a large military presence.[83]

Additionally, because liberal democracies allow their citizens to express their opinion through peaceful demonstrations, anti-base movements can strain an otherwise strong bilateral relationship. For instance, persistent local opposition to the U.S. bases on Okinawa has remained a significant irritant in U.S.-Japanese bilateral relations since 1996.[84] Consequently, maintaining access has become a more demanding and complicated task that requires finding ways to mitigate local opposition and generate grassroots support for a U.S. military presence.

The norm of democracy has become so accepted that increasingly even nondemocratic regimes pretend to abide by it by holding sham elections. While authoritarian leaders are not directly accountable to the public in the same way that democratic leaders are, there is still considerable evidence that they do take into account (and can become entrapped by) domestic public opinion.[85] This is even true in the Middle East, one of the least democratized areas of the world; as Marc Lynch notes, "almost every actor in the region—even if they say the opposite—pays close attention to public opinion and acts as if it matters."[86] Nondemocratic Middle Eastern governments have, for example, prohibited direct combat operations from their territory because of domestic sensitivities.[87]

---

[82] In 1999, the Philippine Senate ratified the Visiting Forces Agreement, which authorized the U.S. military to temporarily deploy to the islands providing U.S. forces were not engaged in combat operations. Thomas Lum, *The Republic of the Philippines and U.S. Interests*, Washington, D.C.: Congressional Research Service, April 5, 2012, p. 14. Section 25 of The Philippine Constitution states "After the expiration in 1991 of the Agreement between the Republic of the Philippines and the United States of America concerning military bases, foreign military bases, troops, or facilities shall not be allowed in the Philippines except under a treaty duly concurred in by the Senate and, when the Congress so requires, ratified by a majority of the votes cast by the people in a national referendum held for that purpose, and recognized as a treaty by the other contracting State." Office of the President of the Philippines, "The 1987 Constitution of the Republic of the Philippines – Article XVIII," the *Official Gazette Online*.

[83] Calder, 2007, pp. 84–85.

[84] Stacie L. Pettyjohn and Alan J. Vick, "Okinawa Remains an Intractable Thorn for US and Japan," *Asia Times Online*, May 25, 2012.

[85] See Michael N. Barnett, *Dialogues in Arab Politics*, New York: Columbia University Press, 1998, pp. 25–27; James Reilly, *Strong Society, Smart State: The Rise of Public Opinion in China's Japan Policy*, New York: Columbia University Press, 2011.

[86] Marc Lynch, "Paint By the Numbers," *The National*, May 29, 2009, accessed on November 1, 2012. For more see Marc Lynch, *Voices of the New Arab Public: Iraq, al-Jazeera, and Middle East Politics Today*, New York: Columbia University Press, 2007.

[87] In the 1990s, many Persian Gulf States would often permit supporting operations to be flown from their territory, but not combat operations. Alfred B. Prados, *Iraq: Former and Recent Military Confrontations*, Washington, D.C.: Congressional Research Service, October 16, 2002, pp. 12–13.

More recently, advancements in communications technologies have provided an additional lever for the public to pressure host governments.[88] Over the past few decades, the diffusion of modern technologies such as satellite television, the Internet, and mobile phones has produced a new information environment that enables the distribution of information, images, and videos to others in a matter of seconds. Previously, knowledge about a U.S. military presence, in particular its negative effects, was primarily limited to neighboring communities. Today, however, technology connects people who are separated by thousands of miles, enabling them to share information about U.S. bases and to hear about others' experiences. Because of this porous information environment, it is increasingly difficult for the United States to conceal an overseas U.S. military presence, or to contain negative publicity about accidents or crimes committed by U.S. military personnel abroad. Additionally, U.S. rivals can use these communications technologies to try to drive a wedge between the United States and a host nation by publicizing negative stories or disinformation about the U.S. military presence.[89] In short, technology enables basing issues that might have been ignored in the past to gain national and international attention, placing greater pressure on host governments to respond. Furthermore, anti-base movements that had been focused on local grievances—either nationalist or pragmatic—now collaborate with other groups in foreign nations, bringing more pressure to bear on the United States and host governments.[90]

As a result of the strengthening norm of sovereignty, the increasing influence of public opinion, and the diffusion of information and communications technologies, U.S. basing rights continue to be whittled away by host nations seeking to protect their sovereignty or to respond to domestic pressures. While most Americans tend to believe "that overseas basing is a legitimate and necessary instrument of U.S. foreign policy," other nations are increasingly questioning this right.[91] As a result of these political challenges, the United States' overseas bases are increasingly "embattled garrisons."[92]

Peacetime Access Risk

There have been a number of nations where protest movements against U.S. bases have not had an adverse impact on U.S. access; for example, Italy.[93] The United States has also faced serious

---

[88] Some view these technological developments as a key part of globalization. Peter J. Katzenstein, *A World of Regions: Asia and Europe in the American Imperium*, Ithaca, N.Y.: Cornell University Press, 2005, p. 13.

[89] We thank reviewer Alexander Cooley for bringing this point to our attention.

[90] Andrew Yeo, "Not In Anyone's Backyard: The Emergence and Identity of a Transnational Anti-Base Network," *International Studies Quarterly*, Vol. 53, No. 3, September 2009, pp. 571–594.

[91] Blaker, 1990, p. 52.

[92] "Embattled Garrisons" is Kent Calder's apt description. See Calder, 2007. Calder, 2007, and Blaker, 1990, each note that there has been a long-term trend of shrinking overseas bases.

[93] For more on Italy, see Andrew Yeo, "Ideas and Institutions in Contentious Politics: Anti-U.S. Base Movements in Ecuador and Italy," *Comparative Politics*, Vol. 42, No. 4, July 2010, pp. 441–446.

public opposition in some locations that has led to reductions in its military presence or other adjustments to its posture; for example the Japanese island of Okinawa and in South Korea.[94] Finally, there are nations that have completely expelled U.S. forces, including the Philippines in 1992 and Uzbekistan in 2005.[95] Given this variation, what explains where access is most reliable and where it is most at risk? We have found that two factors—regime type and access relationship—determine the level of peacetime access risk.[96] By combining these factors, we create a composite risk metric.

Regime Type

A number of studies have highlighted the role that domestic political institutions play in a host nation's propensity to contest U.S. bases, but Alexander Cooley has articulated the most well developed argument of this type.[97] Cooley maintains that different types of regimes—authoritarian, democratizing, or consolidated democratic—vary in their tendency to adhere to international commitments due to the ability of their institutions to "lock in" these agreements.[98] According to Cooley, consolidated democracies, which have procedural legitimacy, institutional stability, and well-developed party systems, are the most dependable host nations; democratizing states are the least dependable host nations; and authoritarian states fall somewhere in between. We modify this argument. When considering the long-term durability of access relationships, we argue that while consolidated democracies are indeed more dependable than other nations, authoritarian states are the least reliable host nations, while democratizing nations are the ones that fall in between. See Table 4.1 for the impact of regime type on access risk.

During the Cold War, authoritarian leaders were seen as steadfast anticommunist allies because of their ability to ignore public opinion and unilaterally provide the United States with access to bases.[99] However, because decisionmaking in an authoritarian state is not constrained by independent institutions, such as a legislature or judiciary, the decision to accept or contest U.S. bases rests with an individual or small group of decisionmakers. In other words, authoritarian leaders who are not bound by the rule of law or constrained by a system of checks and balances can easily rescind American access or capriciously demand that basing agreements be renegotiated. In 1962, for example, King Saud abruptly announced that he was terminating

---

[94] For more on Japan and South Korea, see Yeo, 2011, pp. 118–148; 63–85; Cooley, 2008, pp. 95–174; and Andrew Yeo, "U.S. Military Base Realignment in South Korea," *Peace Review: A Journal of Social Justice,* Vol. 22, No. 2, May 2010, pp. 113–120.

[95] Scott G. Frickenstein, "Kicked Out of K2," *Air Force Magazine*, Vol. 93, No. 9, September 2010; Cooley, 2008, pp. 56–94, 230–232; Yeo, 2011, pp. 35–62.

[96] Calder, 2007, pp. 112–119; Cooley, 2008, pp. 13–18.

[97] While Cooley's argument actually involves two variables—a regime's dependence on the United States for political survival in addition to the contractual credibility of institutions—it is the latter variable that accounts for most of the variation.

[98] Cooley, 2008, p. 16.

[99] Cooley, 2008, pp. 14–15; Calder, 2007, pp. 115–119.

the United States' lease to Dhahran airfield. Since World War II, the United States had invested substantial resources into transforming Dhahran into one of the largest air bases in the world so that it could support U.S. bombers. Nevertheless, the Saudi monarch determined that because of revolutionary turmoil in the Arab world, "Dhahran was too politically costly for the kingdom to maintain."[100]

Table 4.1. Regime Type and Peacetime Access Risk

Regime Type	Impact on Basing Agreements	Access Risk
Consolidated democracy	Legitimate agreements Established party system moderates officials' positions on bases Technocratic administration of agreement routinizes U.S. presence	Low
Democratizing	Previous agreement lacks legitimacy Weak institutions lead candidates to appeal to nationalism, politicizing U.S. bases Opportunity to forge a more equitable and legitimate agreement	Medium
Authoritarian	Agreements lack popular legitimacy Unconstrained decision making enables leaders to make sudden changes to U.S. access Contingent on the leader who made agreement Unlikely to persist beyond the regime	High

In addition to the instability caused by a personalized decisionmaking process, bases in authoritarian states are at risk because they are may not endure beyond the regime that makes an agreement. This combined with the fact that authoritarian regimes are the most likely to be suddenly overthrown, either in a coup or by a democratic revolution, makes basing in authoritarian states dangerous. More importantly, when a dictator has been toppled (either by another authoritarian ruler or in a popular revolution), the new regime has almost invariably contested a preexisting American military presence to bolster its popular support by demonstrating a break with its predecessor.[101] In part, this is due to the fact that despite pronouncements to the contrary, the existence of U.S. bases in authoritarian states suggests that the United States is actively encouraging or at least tacitly condoning autocratic repression to advance American security interests.[102] In Bahrain today, for example, many assume that the U.S. government supports the Al-Khalifa regime's efforts to repress demonstrators to ensure

---

[100] Rachel Bronson, *Thicker Than Oil: America's Uneasy Partnership with Saudi Arabia*, Oxford, UK: Oxford University Press, 2008, p. 79.

[101] Calder, 2007, pp. 112–114.

[102] Gerson, 1991, p. 17.

continued access to the base used by the USN's 5th Fleet.[103] The United States can be tainted by its support for autocrats, making it difficult, if not impossible, to secure access in the future.

For instance, Libyan revolutionary leader Muammar Qaddafi wasted little time before expelling the United States from Wheelus Air Base after deposing King Idris in 1969. Because foreign bases were seen as an extension of colonialism, the U.S. and British military presence, which was established in Libya during World War II, was universally unpopular. Over time, opposition to the foreign bases had steadily grown due to nationalist resentment over the perceived affront to Libya's sovereignty. Libyan nationalists also took umbrage at the fact that foreign bases perpetuated the nation's economic dependence by making the state reliant on the base rents. As a result of these sentiments, once in power, Qaddafi took the widely popular step of forcing the Americans and the British to abandon their military facilities in Libya by 1970.[104]

The perception that the United States is actively backing an authoritarian regime is reinforced if dictators and their cronies personally profit from the presence of U.S. bases.[105] In Kyrgyzstan, for example, there is the widespread belief that the United States awarded fuel contracts to companies run by family members of the past two presidents as a bribe to preserve U.S. access to the air base at Manas. The perceived corruption and fraud at Manas contributed to the discontent that fueled popular revolutions in Kyrgyzstan in 2005 and 2010, and embittered the Kyrgyz population toward the United States.[106] In sum, an American military presence in autocratic regimes inevitably associates the United States with unpopular authoritarian regimes and oppression, often leading to blowback if the regime falls.

By contrast, although democratizing nations may politicize and restrict U.S. basing rights in the short term, over the long run a stable and enduring (albeit less robust) form of access can still emerge. Democratization is generally seen as a core U.S. interest, but it is usually detrimental to U.S. basing rights—at least in the short term—because the onset of political contestation in nations with weak institutions encourages leaders to appeal to nationalism to garner public support.[107] In this setting, basing agreements that were made under authoritarian regimes are

---

[103] Alexander Cooley and Daniel H. Nexon, "Bahrain's Base Politics: The Arab Spring and America's Military Bases," *Foreignaffairs.com*, April 5, 2011.

[104] Alison Pargeter, *Libya the Rise and Fall of Qaddafi*, New Haven, Conn.: Yale University Press, 2012, pp. 44–46, 71.

[105] Cooley, 2008, pp. 249–250.

[106] Initially, the fuel contracts were awarded to companies (Mina and Red Star) run by President Askar Akayev's son and his son-in-law. After a popular revolution forced Akayev out in 2005 because of alleged corruption, his successor, President Kurmanbek Bakiyev, and his son expropriated the two fuel subcontractors that continued to receive U.S. contracts. U.S. House of Representatives, *Mystery at Manas: Strategic Blind Spots in the Department of Defense's Fuel Contracts In Kyrgyzstan*, Washington, D.C.: Report of the Majority Staff, Subcommittee on National Security and Foreign Affairs, Committee on Oversight and Government, December 2010, pp. 13–14.

[107] Cooley, 2008, pp. 16–18. According to Cooley democratizing nations are those that are "undergoing a democratic transition from authoritarian rule" (Cooley, 2008, p. 16). Yet a democratic transition is only "the interval between one political regime and another." O'Donnell, Guillermo, and Philippe Schmitter, "Tentative Conclusions About Uncertain Democracies," in Guillermo O'Donnell, Philippe Schmitter, and Laurence Whitehead, eds.,

viewed as illegitimate because they were not popularly ratified. As the political system opens up, elites must suddenly compete for popular support and frequently end up in a nationalist bidding war. In this environment, denouncing U.S. bases becomes an attractive and effective way to win popular support because anti-base rhetoric taps into existing nationalist and pragmatic grievances. Consequently, in democratizing states, candidates for office will frequently demand that basing rights be renegotiated on more favorable terms or that U.S. access be abrogated altogether. Once in office, however, candidates who called for radical changes to U.S. basing rights often balk at following through on these promises due to the financial benefits or the security guarantees that their nation would lose. Nevertheless, these leaders might find themselves trapped by their own anti-base rhetoric and forced to follow through on their campaign pledges—at least partially—or risk losing credibility.[108] In sum, in democratizing states electoral incentives make U.S. bases a politicized and strongly contested issue that typically results in lost or significantly diminished U.S. access.

For example, after Greece reverted back to democracy in 1974, U.S. basing rights became a hotly contested national issue that dominated bilateral relations for nearly a decade. This was due to the fact that during a period of authoritarian rule between 1964 and 1974, geostrategic considerations encouraged the U.S. government to maintain close relations—including a number of high-ranking official visits—with the Greek government despite its undemocratic character. As a result, many Greeks suspected that the United States had orchestrated the military's 1967 takeover.[109] After the disastrous Turkish invasion of Cyprus, the Greek military stepped down, and free and fair elections were held in November 1974. The new prime minister, Constantine Karamanlis, announced that Greece would seek a new basing agreement that was established on the principles of "national independence, security for the country and national dignity"[110] Consequently, Karamanlis stressed that the United States could only retain bases that were used for mutual defense and that it would have to abandon the facilities that only served U.S. interests. After difficult negotiations, the United States was allowed to retain access to its existing bases, which were transferred to Greek command, in return for a hefty aid package. However,

---

Transitions from Authoritarian Rule, Part 4, Baltimore, Md.: Johns Hopkins University Press, 1986, p. 6. Because Cooley's case studies suggest that democratization can last for decades, well after a new regime has taken power, it seems that his real argument is that nonconsolidated democracies—not just states in the midst of a transition—are unreliable hosts. To avoid confusion, we maintain Cooley's usage of the word democratizing, but actually mean nonconsolidated democracies.

[108] A similar mechanism of nationalist outbidding is used to explain other international outcomes in Jack Snyder, *Myths of Empire: Domestic Politics and International Ambition*, Ithaca, N.Y.: Cornell University Press, 1993; Jack Snyder and Karen Ballentine, "Nationalism and the Marketplace of Ideas," *International Security*, Vol. 21, No. 2, Fall 1996; Jack L. Snyder, *From Voting to Violence: Democratization and Nationalist Conflict*, New York: W. W. Norton & Company, 2000; Edward D. Mansfield and Jack Snyder, *Electing to Fight: Why Emerging Democracies Go to War*, Cambridge, Mass.: MIT Press, 2005.

[109] F. Stephen Larrabee, "Athens: Greece for the Greeks," *Foreign Policy*, Vol. 45, Winter 1981–1982, p. 160.

[110] Quoted in Steven V. Roberts, "Greece to Allow Most U.S. Bases," *New York Times*, December 13, 1974.

Karamanlis scuttled an agreement that the Nixon administration had reached with the Greek junta to homeport the 6th Fleet at the port of Elefsis.[111]

U.S. basing rights remained highly politicized during the premiership of Andreas Papandreou, the leader of the Pan-Hellenic Socialist Movement (PASOK). In 1981, Papandreou ran a populist campaign appealing to Greek nationalism with the slogan "Greece now belongs to the Greeks."[112] As a candidate, Papandreou argued that Greece should "refuse to recognize military agreements particularly with American imperialism"[113] and that "foreign bases have no place in our country."[114] Despite this fiery rhetoric, once in office Papandreou was slow to address the basing issue and eventually reopened the base negotiations rather than unilaterally revoke U.S. access. Then, in 1983, the United States and Greece reached a Defense and Economic Cooperation Agreement that extended U.S. basing rights for five years. The United States viewed the agreement as potentially allowing future access, while the Greek government publicly maintained that the agreement terminated U.S. access in five years.[115] Despite his public position, privately Papandreou realized that his nation desperately needed the U.S. economic and military support that it received for the bases, but his nationalist rhetoric had unleashed popular forces that he found difficult to control. Papandreou, therefore, took the contradictory actions of repeatedly announcing that U.S. bases would be closed imminently even as he temporarily extended U.S. access.[116]

In contrast to democratizing states where U.S. bases are contested and highly politicized, U.S. bases are generally accepted in consolidated democracies.[117] Three features of consolidated democracies make them dependable host nations.[118] First, basing agreements reached by democratic governments are viewed as legitimate because they have been negotiated by freely elected leaders and/or ratified by a legislature or through a public referendum, which helps to defuse nationalist backlash. Second, consolidated democracies have stable institutions with

---

[111] Sandars, 2000, pp. 263–264.

[112] Quoted in Akis Kalaitzidis and Nikolaos Zahariadis, "Papandreou's NATO Policy: Continuity or Change?" *Journal of the Hellenic Diaspora*, Vol. 23, No. 1, 1997, p. 107.

[113] Quoted in John C. Loulis, "Papandreou's Foreign Policy," *Foreign Affairs*, Vol. 63, No. 2, Winter 1984, p. 378.

[114] Quoted in Stephen Webbe, "US Ponders Possible Loss of Military Bases in Greece," *Christian Science Monitor*, October 20, 1981.

[115] Richard F. Grimmett, *U.S. Military Installations in NATO's Southern Region*, Washington, D.C.: U.S. Government Printing Office, 1986, pp. 36–39.

[116] Sandars, 2000, pp. 266–269.

[117] According to Linz and Stepan, a regime is a consolidated democracy when the "institutions, rules, and patterned incentives and disincentives has become, in a phrase 'the only game in town.'" Juan J. Linz and Alfred Stepan, "Toward Consolidated Democracies," *Journal of Democracy*, Vol. 7, No. 2, 1996.

[118] Cooley, 2008, pp. 15–18. For more on contractual credibility, see Charles Lipson, *Reliable Partners: How Democracies Have Made a Separate Peace*, Princeton, N.J.: Princeton University Press, 2003; and Lisa L. Martin, *Democratic Commitments: Legislatures and International Cooperation*, Princeton, N.J.: Princeton University Press, 2000.

clearly delineated responsibilities. As a result, technocrats are in charge of basing issues, which helps to routinize and depoliticize the matter. Additionally, the involvement of multiple bureaucracies increases the number of actors invested in U.S. bases, making it more difficult to change policies. Third, consolidated democracies have a well-developed party system that pushes politicians to temper their positions. In democratizing states, candidates often resort to nationalist and populist promises to get elected, while in consolidated democracies, party systems moderate the views of candidates and elected officials.

In sum, consolidated democracies that are characterized by procedural legitimacy, institutional stability, and well-regulated political competition are the most reliable partners and host nations, because they cannot arbitrarily modify or abandon their agreements. This does not mean a complete absence of opposition to a U.S. military presence, but rather that basing rights are not a highly charged national political issue. Local pragmatic opposition to U.S. bases might persist, but it typically remains contained and is unlikely to change national policy. Incidents related to U.S. bases—such as a plane crash or a crime committed by U.S. military personnel— can temporarily gain significant attention, but their impact tends to be fleeting. Outside of these infrequent high-profile incidents, U.S. bases tend to recede from the national political discourse because of the particular institutional features of consolidated democracies.

To understand the calming effect of democratic consolidation on basing rights, it is helpful to return to the issue of U.S. bases in Greece in the mid-1980s. Once in office, Papandreou backed away from his campaign pledge to close the U.S. bases. Moreover, as Greek democracy matured, U.S. basing rights became depoliticized and generally accepted. For instance, in 1989 Papandreou's successor, Constantine Mitsotakis, ran on a platform of upholding the basing agreement with the United States. However, as the Cold War came to an end, the United States determined that many of its bases in Greece were no longer necessary. Eventually, DoD withdrew from all of its bases in Greece except for Souda Bay; since the 1980s, the U.S. presence in Greece has not provoked great controversy.[119]

Another example that helps to illustrate the resiliency of basing rights in consolidated democracies is Italy. During the Cold War, Italy was one of the most reliable host nations, as it never attempted to renegotiate its original basing agreement with the United States.[120] Nevertheless, there were a few basing-related incidents that created tension in the U.S.-Italian relationship, but ultimately had only a limited impact on U.S. peacetime access. For example, in 1985 during the *Achille Lauro* affair, U.S. forces overstepped their bounds as they attempted to detain the Palestinian terrorists who had hijacked a cruise liner and killed an American citizen. The Italian government had authorized the U.S. fighter jets that had intercepted the plane carrying the terrorists to land at the naval airfield at Sigonella. Once on the ground, U.S. forces claimed that they had the right to arrest the terrorists, but Italy correctly argued that the United

[119] Sandars, 2000, p. 268.

[120] Sandars, 2000, p. 228.

States did not have jurisdiction in this instance, eventually forcing the United States to concede on this point. As a result of this incident, Italy announced that its bases could only be used for NATO missions.[121] However, the U.S.-Italian relationship quickly rebounded from the *Achille Lauro* affair, and in 1988 Italy offered to host the USAF F-16s that were being evicted from Torrejon AB in Spain. More recently, U.S. basing rights have weathered significant local opposition to the expansion of the U.S. Army base at Vicenza.[122]

Access Relationships

While regime type influences the reliability of peacetime access, arguments that focus solely on domestic politics are incomplete because they ignore ideational and strategic variables in addition to bargaining incentives that can either contain or exacerbate domestic political opposition.[123] We argue that a second variable—the type of access relationship—captures these different factors and significantly impacts the level of peacetime access risk. Although the decision to provide the United States with access is often multifaceted, the primary factor often falls into one of three categories: a deep security consensus (enduring partnership), a shared perception of threat (mutual defense), or a desire for material benefits (transactional). Table 4.2 shows the different type of access relationships and the attendant level of access risk.

Table 4.2. Type of Access Relationship and Peacetime Access Risk

Type of Access Relationship	Host Nation Motive for Providing Access	Effect on Access	Access Risk
Enduring Partnership	Elite security consensus	Depoliticized	Low
Mutual Defense	Perception of shared threat	Stable for facing common threat	Medium
Transactional	Material benefits	Volatile	High

Transactional Relationships

In the transactional model, a country makes bases on its territory available to the United States to secure material benefits.[124] In this situation, compensation may take many forms, including

---

[121] Sandars, 2000, pp. 233–235; Grimmett, 1986, pp. 22–24.

[122] Cooley, 2008, pp. 207–210. For more on protests to the expansion at Vicenza see Yeo, 2011, pp. 100–116.

[123] Yeo, 2011, p. 187.

[124] Pettyjohn, 2012, pp. 103–104. A number of studies of U.S. overseas bases have asserted that the transactional model is predominant, but these studies typically focus on negotiations after the base has already been established. They therefore neglect a critically important part of the life cycle of an overseas base: why and under what terms it is initially created. By doing so, they underestimate the importance of security interests in driving the original basing agreement. See Cooley, 2008, pp. 46–47; Cooley and Spruyt, 2009, pp. 103–111; Blaker, 1989, pp. 105–114; Calder, 2007, pp. 127–140, 136–148; and Duncan L. Clarke and Daniel O'Connor, "U.S. Base Rights Payments After the Cold War," *Orbis*, Vol. 37, No. 3, Summer 1993. By contrast, Harkavy, 1989, pp. 320–358, argues that

straightforward rent payments, economic assistance, or arms sales. Compensation-driven access creates an unstable dynamic because the host nation has an incentive to highlight the problems associated with an American military presence in an effort to extract larger payments. In particular, the host government emphasizes its domestic constraints, namely public opposition to a U.S. military presence, to gain leverage in negotiations with the United States and ultimately to secure more compensation.[125]

In a transactional relationship, a host nation will attempt to take advantage of any missteps by U.S. forces—either accidents or crimes committed by U.S. personnel—to obtain a better deal. Because the negotiations are iterative, transactional agreements will be characterized by contracts with increasingly short timelines, which enables the host government to frequently renegotiate. In addition, a host government might try to intentionally enflame nationalist sentiment and encourage popular demonstrations to strengthen its bargaining leverage, especially in the lead-up to or during basing negotiations. Although the federal government might engineer or encourage nationalist outrage, domestic opposition to transactional basing agreements is also likely to emerge organically[126] because it is clear that the bases serve the interests of the United States more so than those of the host nation. However, if a host government attempts to generate opposition to U.S. bases, it risks becoming entrapped by its own rhetoric and may be forced to follow through on its bluffs to limit or terminate U.S. access. Consequently, transactional basing agreements typically result in a vicious bargaining cycle, escalating payments, and restrictions on (or the loss of) access.[127]

The epitome of the transaction model is Kyrgyzstan, which provided the United States with access to Manas AB (later renamed the Transit Center at Manas) beginning in 2001. U.S. payments have taken numerous forms, including economic assistance, and have dramatically

---

mutual security interests were dominant for the first several decades of the Cold War but that, more recently, access relationships are becoming more transactional.

[125] Robert D. Putnam, "Diplomacy and Domestic Politics: the Logic of Two-Level Games," *International Organization*, Vol. 42, No. 3, Summer 1988, p. 450.

[126] An unusual and perhaps unique hybrid is the triangular transactional model found in Okinawa. The people of Okinawa experienced massive destruction and loss of life following the U.S. amphibious landing in April 1945. During the battle, they felt abandoned and exploited by the Japanese government; during the occupation by the U.S. (lasting from 1945 to 1972), Okinawans were resentful of U.S. relocation and land use policies as well as the large U.S. military presence. By 1972, when the United States returned Okinawa to Japanese control, strong pacifist views and resentment toward Tokyo and Washington had become the norm in Okinawa. Since 1972, Tokyo has provided compensation to Okinawa via rent payments to individual landowners, major infrastructure projects at the local level, and other financial aid at both the local and prefecture levels. In this model, Washington provides security benefits to Tokyo, Tokyo provides financial compensation to Naha (the capital of Okinawa), and Naha provides access to the United States. The compensation dynamics are largely the same as discussed earlier, except in this case when there are accidents or criminal behavior associated with U.S. forces, Naha complains to Tokyo and Tokyo compensates. For more on the incentives that Tokyo provides, see Alexander Cooley and Kimberly Marten, "Base Motives: the Political Economy of Okinawa's Antimilitarism," *Armed Forces and* Society, Vol. 32, No. 4, 2006, Cooley, 2008; pp. 135–159; Calder, 2007, pp. 166–175.

[127] This is similar to what Calder calls baazar-type basing. Calder, 2007, pp. 140–151.

escalated from their initial levels. The 2001 basing agreement obligated the United States to pay an annual $2 million lease payment in addition to takeoff and landing fees. The United States also awarded lucrative fuel contracts to companies run by relatives of President Askar Akayev. Once U.S. forces were thrown out of Uzbekistan in November 2005, Kurmanbek Bakiyev, who won the presidency after Kyrgyzstan's Tulip Revolution in 2005, sensed that he could take advantage of the United States' increased dependence on Manas to demand a new deal. Bakiyev accused the United States of only paying a pittance of what Manas was worth and threatened to expel U.S. forces unless Washington paid a "hundredfold" increase in rent.[128] Consequently, in July 2006, the rent for Manas was increased to $17 million per year and the United States provided more than $150 million in other types of assistance during 2007.

This agreement held until February 2009, when Bakiyev declared that he was closing Manas and that Kyrgyzstan was receiving over $2 billion from Russia, which seemed interested in securing access to the airbase (or at least denying the United States access). This announcement set off a bidding war between Moscow and Washington, with Bakiyev playing each country off the other by accepting $300 million from Russia before ultimately renegotiating the Manas lease with the United States.[129] The basing agreement announced in 2009 again raised the lease payments to $60 million per year, and, by FY 2011, the United States was paying $150.6 million.[130] In June 2013, the Kyrgyz parliament voted to terminate U.S. access to Manas in July 2014, when the current agreement expired.[131] Despite this development, negotiations over extending U.S. access to Manas continue. It remains to be seen, therefore, whether Kyrgyz President Almazbek Atambaev will uphold his promise to establish a civilian transportation hub at Manas or if these statements are simply a negotiating tactic.[132]

Mutual Defense Relationships

In the second model, nations offer to host American forces when there is common threat.[133] This is a fairly stable foundation for a basing agreement so long as the U.S. military presence remains focused on countering this mutual security challenge. The perception of a shared and growing threat is the most frequent reason that other nations consent to the establishment of a peacetime

---

[128] Quoted in Cooley, 2008, pp. 232–234.

[129] Alexander Cooley, "Manas Hysteria: Why the United States Can't Keep Buying Off Kyrgyz Leaders to Keep Its Vital Air Base Open," *Foreignpolicy.com*, April 12, 2010; Alexander Cooley, *Great Games, Local Rules; The New Great Power Contest in Central Asia*, Oxford, UK: Oxford University Press, 2012, pp. 121–127.

[130] The FY 2011 payments consisted of a $60 million lease payment, $27.4 million in landing and other fees, a $30 million contribution to Kyrgyz Aeronavigation, $30.9 million for infrastructural improvements, $824,000 for programmatic humanitarian assistance, and $1.4 million for other local spending. Cooley, 2008, pp. 233–234; Jim Nichol, *Kyrgyzstan: Recent Developments and U.S. Interests*, Washington, D.C.: Congressional Research Service, January 19, 2012, p. 13

[131] Olga Dzyubenko, "Russian Ally Kyrgyzstan Set U.S. Air Base Closure Deadline," *Reuters*, June 20, 2013.

[132] John Vandiver, "US Seeking Extension of Manas Air Base Lease," *Stars and Stripes*, January 16, 2013.

[133] Pettyjohn, 2012, pp. 102–103.

U.S. military presence. During the early years of the Cold War, for instance, many nations remained unconvinced that the Soviet Union posed a threat to them; consequently, the Truman administration encountered problems securing long-term basing rights. The outbreak of the Korean war in June 1950 dispelled this uncertainty and led many Western European states that had previously resisted the creation of U.S. bases on their territory to welcome U.S. forces.

Similarly, increasingly aggressive Iranian actions impelled a number of states in the Persian Gulf, including the UAE, to provide U.S. forces with access to their military facilities. As a result of increased regional tensions during the tanker war in 1988, the UAE hosted temporary USN and USMC deployments for the first time. Yet it was not until Saddam Hussein invaded Kuwait in August 1990 that U.S. forces were permitted to remain in the Emirates for an extended period of time. The UAE was less concerned with Iraq than with the growing challenge posed by Iran, and the Emirates saw the United States as the only actor interested in and capable of checking Iranian power.[134] Consequently, in 1992, the United States reached an agreement with the UAE for access to air and naval facilities—an agreement that was expanded in 1994. Today, the USAF maintains a continuous rotational presence in the UAE, which fluctuates depending upon the level of threat. For instance, as tensions rose over Iran's nuclear program during the spring of 2012, the United States reportedly deployed some of its most advanced fighters—F-22 Raptors—to Al-Dhafra AB.[135]

In this type of mutual defense relationship, however, the United States is likely to encounter difficulties if it tries to use bases or forces for unrelated operations.[136] During the Cold War, for example, many European allies refused to allow the United States to use bases in their countries for non-NATO operations, including the 1973 U.S. airlift to Israel and the 1986 strike against Libya.[137] Similarly, the South Korean government has opposed efforts by the United States to deploy its forces from the peninsula for other operations.[138] Moreover, if a host nation's threat perception declines or diverges from that of the United States, basing rights can become

---

[134] Kenneth Katzman, *The United Arab Emirates (UAE): Issues for U.S. Policy*, Washington, D.C.: Congressional Research Service, October 4, 2012, p. 10. For more details on the early U.S. presence in the UAE, see Anthony H. Cordesman, *Bahrain, Oman, Qatar and the UAE, Challenges of Security*, Boulder, Colo.: Westview Press, 1997, p. 378.

[135] Katzman, 2012, p. 10.

[136] During the Cold War, when the United States wanted to use its European bases or the forces stationed at these facilities for other operations, it often encountered resistance. See Grimmett, 1986; Walter J. Boyne, "El Dorado Canyon," *Air Force Magazine*, Vol. 82, No. 3, March 1999; and Adam B. Siegel, *Basing and Other Constraints on Ground-Based Aviation Contributions to U.S. Contingency Operations*, Washington, D.C.: Center for Naval Analysis, March 1995.

[137] During Operation Nickel Grass—the 1973 airlift to Israel—Portugal allowed U.S. aircraft to use Lajes Air Base in the Azores, while for Operation El Dorado Canyon—the 1986 strike against Libya—the UK permitted U.S. aircraft stationed in Britain to carry out the strike, but Spain and France denied overflight for this mission. Grimmett 1986, and Siegel, 1995.

[138] Mark E. Manyin, Emma Chanlett-Avery, and Mary Beth Nikitin, *U.S.–South Korea Relations*, Washington, D.C.: Congressional Research Service, November 28, 2011, p. 22.

increasingly tenuous, and access is more likely to be rescinded.[139] By the mid-1970s, the fears of communist expansion had greatly receded, particularly in nations that faced more proximate regional threats, such as Greece and Turkey. After the July 1974 Turkish invasion of Cyprus, the Greek and Turkish governments were more concerned about each other than the Soviet Union, and they realized that the United States would not come to their defense against another member of NATO. Consequently, the perception of shared threat disappeared, and each country continued to host U.S. forces only because they needed U.S. aid and military support to defend themselves against their Mediterranean rival.[140]

Today, there is no longer any single, overriding, and unambiguous global threat akin to the Soviet Union during the Cold War. Because communism was viewed as a threat to much of the world during this period, the United States not only had access to many overseas bases, it also had considerable freedom of action in how it used those bases. Specifically, host nations often allowed U.S. forces to use their facilities for operations in different theaters as long as they were helping to check the communist threat. While the United States confronts a variety of threats in different regions, however, most other nations today face geographically discrete challenges.[141] Moreover, because the United States often seeks access arrangements that enable it to use bases for a range of different operations, it is more difficult to create a direct and enduring tie between U.S. bases and the security of a host nation, which complicates obtaining and preserving access.[142] Many nations are also hesitant to allow U.S. forces to be stationed on their soil to counter unspecified future threats because the host nation will be implicated in any operations that these forces conduct.[143] As a result, the United States is likely to find that the mutual defense model yields more restricted access in comparison to the Cold War.[144]

---

[139] Pettyjohn, 2012, pp. 104–105; Stephen Walt, *The Origins of Alliances*, Ithaca, N.Y.: Cornell University Press, 1987; Calder, 2007, pp. 69–72.

[140] Sandars, 2000, pp. 264–267, 275–279.

[141] The war on terrorism that was launched after 9/11 provided an initial basis for mutual defense, but the threat has tended to be more localized than during the Cold War. Moreover, at times the United States has found itself deeply involved in local political disputes because a host government manipulated the parameters of the war on terrorism to bolster its position internally. For example, Uzbek President Islam Karimov used the war on terrorism as a guise to crack down on all types of dissent. Cooley, 2008, pp. 224–226.

[142] Andrew Krepinevich and Robert O. Work, *A New Global Defense Posture for the Transoceanic Era*, Washington, D.C.: Center for Strategic and Budgetary Assessments, 2007, p. 190.

[143] Lincoln P. Bloomfield, Jr., "Politics and Diplomacy of the Global Defense Posture Review," in Carnes Lord, ed., *Reposituring the Force: U.S. Overseas Presence in the Twenty-First Century*, Newport, R.I.: Naval War College Press, 2006, pp. 61–62.

[144] Another potential difference between the mutual defense model today and the Cold War is the duration of the threat. If shared threats do not persist for decades, such a relationship may not produce an identity change and therefore may not create enduring partnerships.

Finally, there is the enduring partnership model. All of the countries that fall into this category had initially granted the United States basing rights for a reason (either shared threat or compensation) that has since disappeared.[145] Yet, these nations have continued to host U.S. forces because of an elite security consensus that the U.S. military plays a stabilizing role in the world and that the host nation has broad shared interests that are advanced by hosting U.S. forces.[146] Shared threat can contribute to the development of a strong security consensus, but other factors, such as common values, identity, and history, also play an important role, resulting in ties that are more durable than just mutual defense.[147] For instance, today NATO is founded upon a "collective identity of liberal democracies," which generally supports a continued U.S. military presence in Europe.[148]

There is considerable evidence that the general public's views on U.S. bases do not determine a host government's policy toward a U.S. military presence.[149] For instance, public opinion polls in the Philippines in the years prior to 1991 regularly found that a majority of those surveyed supported U.S. bases.[150] Nevertheless, in 1991 the Philippine Senate failed to ratify a treaty that would have extended U.S. basing rights, resulting in the expulsion of U.S. forces. There is, therefore, an imperfect correlation between public opinion and host government basing decisions, which in part can be explained by the degree of agreement among elites about their nation's relationship with the United States.[151] When there is a strong security consensus, host

---

[145] This is similar to the notion of alliance persistence. "An alliance is said to 'persist' when it is renewed or continued even after the initial conditions that gave rise to it have disappeared or been so transformed as to eliminate the original need." Stephen M. Walt, "Why Alliances Endure or Collapse," *Survival*, Vol. 39, No. 1, 1997, p. 134.

[146] Elites are defined as foreign and defense policy opinion leaders. This is a broad group of people, including government officials, politicians, members of the diplomatic corps or defense establishment, academics, and policy analysts. Yeo, 2011, pp. 14–15.

[147] This is not to suggest collective beliefs cannot change, but they tend to be fairly durable. For more on how norms and identities can change, see Paul Kowert and Jeffery Legro, "Norms, Identity, and Their Limits: A Theoretical Reprise," in Peter J. Katzenstein, ed., *The Culture of National Security: Norms and Identity in World Politics*, New York: Columbia University Press, 1996, pp. 470–474, 488–490.

[148] Thomas Risse-Kappen, "Collective Identity in a Democratic Community: The Case of NATO," in Katzenstein, 1996, p. 395. Going even farther, Monteleone claims that Europeans do not perceive U.S. bases to be a threat or a violation of their sovereignty because of the existence of a Euro-Atlantic pluralistic security community. Carla Monteleone, "The Evolution of the Euro-Atlantic Pluralistic Security Community: Impact and Perspectives of the Presence of American Bases in Italy," *Journal of Transatlantic Studies*, Vol. 5, No. 1, 2007, p. 69.

[149] Cooley examines public opinion polls across time in a number of key host nations. See Cooley, 2008, pp. 260–261. Yeo also notes that there are numerous instances in which anti-base movements have successfully mobilized, but have failed to change policy. Yeo, 2011, pp. 12–13. Calder points out there is typically a divergence between elite and general public opinion. Calder, 2007, p. 67.

[150] For example, in a poll taken in August of 1988 in the Philippines, 74 percent of the respondents wanted U.S. bases to stay, 18 percent wanted them closed, and 6 percent were undecided. Walden Bello, "Moment of Decision: The Philippines, the Pacific, and the U.S. Bases," in Gerson and Birchard, 1991, pp. 158–159.

[151] Realists have long argued that the public's views on foreign policy can be manipulated because these foreign affairs are not particularly important to normal people, they have little knowledge about the issues, and their views

nation elites are able to contain anti-base movements that might emerge, preventing them from gaining enough traction to alter national policy. In an effort to defuse anti-base movements, elites can use a variety of strategies, including campaigns to shape public opinion or co-option. As long as elite solidarity persists, enduring partners are likely to successfully minimize the impact of anti-base movements, resulting in only small changes in basing policy (compared with severe limitations or the loss of access).[152] Consequently, this is the most stable type of access relationship, and therefore, ideally, the United States would only create strategic anchors at enduring partner bases. That is not to say that the enduring partner may not grant the United States permission to use a base for a particular operation or that the relationship is entirely trouble-free, but in general it offers the most secure type of peacetime access.

All of the United States' enduring partners provided basing access during the Cold War, and continued to do so after the dissolution of the Soviet Union in 1991. Because the Soviet Union was the shared threat that yielded many of the United States' overseas bases, it is not surprising that the end of the Cold War often precipitated the shift into the enduring partnership model, which demonstrates that basing relationships are not static. Instead, over time a host nation's rationale can change, shifting from one type of access relationship to another. (See Table 4.3 for examples.)

The exemplar of the enduring partner model is the United Kingdom, which values the stabilizing role that the United States plays in the world. As a result there is extensive UK-U.S. security cooperation that includes hosting U.S. forces not only in Britain, but also on other British territories such as Diego Garcia, Ascension Island, and RAF Akrotiri.[153]

Moreover, the British government has assiduously worked to contain anti-base movements that have emerged; in particular, it has used a variety of means to deflect challenges to the base on the Indian Ocean atoll of Diego Garcia.[154] There have been two primary challenges to Diego Garcia:[155] the Mauritian government has disputed British sovereignty over the Chagos archipelago, which includes Diego Garcia, and the Chagossians—the islanders that resided on

---

frequently change. The security consensus argument identifies the conditions under which elites may be able to contain or influence public opinion on a U.S. military presence. For more on public opinion, see Ole Rudolf Holsti, *Public Opinion and American Foreign Policy*, Revised Edition, Ann Arbor, Mich.: University of Michigan Press, 2004; and Matthew A. Baum and Philip B. K. Potter, "The Relationship Between Mass Media, Public Opinion, and Foreign Policy: Towards a Theoretical Synthesis," *Annual Review of Political Science*, Vol. 11, No. 39, 2008, pp. 39–65.

[152] Yeo, 2011, pp. 25–27.

[153] Akrotiri is on Cyprus but the British retain sovereign rights over the base. Sandars, 2000, p. 104.

[154] In the 1980s, the British also worked to defuse the protests aimed at bases where U.S. nuclear weapons resided. For more on the British protest movement, see David Heller and Hans Lammerant, "U.S. Nuclear Weapons Bases in Europe," in Catherine Lutz, 2009, pp. 98–102.

[155] This section draws on work that Professor Judy Krutky conducted during a 2012 summer/fall sabbatical at RAND. Judy Krutky, "Can/Should the U.S. Base on Diego Garcia be Maintained? Background and Current Positions of Key Stakeholders," unpublished manuscript, December 2012.

the atoll—have contested the legality of their forcible removal in 1971 and have sought the right to return to the island.[156] Despite mounting pressure in the form of numerous cases in British and international courts, the British government has steadfastly defended its right to the island and taken steps to prevent the islanders return to Diego Garcia.[157]

Table 4.3. Examples of Different Access Relationships

	Transactional Model	Mutual Defense Model	Enduring Partnership
United Kingdom		1946–1990	1991–present
Australia		1955–1990	1991–present
UAE		1990–present	
Djibouti	2002–present		
Kyrgyzstan	2001–present		
Japan		1951–1990	1991–present
Philippines	1956–1992	2001–present	

Measuring Peacetime Access Risk

We have found that the variables regime type and access relationship interact with each other, and that particular combinations are especially stable or volatile (see Table 4.4 for examples). For instance, to date all of the United States' enduring partners have been consolidated democracies, producing an especially durable foundation for peacetime access (see Table 4.4). Well-entrenched democratic institutions make it difficult for governments to modify or abandon existing basing agreements, while the shared identity fostered by a common form of government embeds U.S. access in a broader set of security cooperation activities, helping to depoliticize the issue of U.S. bases.

---

[156] For more on these claims, see David Vine, *Island of Shame: The Secret History of the U.S. Military Base on Diego Garcia*, Princeton, N.J.: Princeton University Press, 2009; and Peter H. Sand, *United States and Britain in Diego Garcia: The Future of a Controversial Base*, New York: Palgrave Macmillan, 2009.

[157] These measures include two royal decrees (orders in council) in June 2004 as well as the decision in April 2010 to establish a Marine Protection Area (MPA) around the Chagos archipelago (excluding Diego Garcia). While the British government denies that it had ulterior motives, opponents contend that the MPA—which prohibits fishing around the atolls—effectively precludes the return of the Chagossians to Diego Garcia because it eliminates their main livelihood. Jon Lunn, "The Chagos Islanders," London, UK: Library House of Commons, April 20, 2012, p. 15; and David Vine and Laura Jeffery, "'Give Us back Diego Garcia': Unity and Division Among Activists in the Indian Ocean," in Lutz, 2009, p. 200.

Table 4.4. Regime Type and Access Relationship Combined

	Enduring Partnership	Mutual Defense	Transactional
Consolidated Democracy	UK 1991-2013 Germany 1991–2013 Spain 1988–2013 Portugal 1996–2013	Romania 2001–2013 South Korea 2004–2013 UK 1946–1990 *France 1952–1967	Portugal 1988–1995 Greece 1990–1998
Democratizing	None	Japan 1951–1969 South Korea 1988–2004 Philippines 2000–2013 *Thailand 1973–75	*Philippines 1986–1992 *Ecuador 1999–2009 Greece 1976–1989 Turkey 1980–2013 Portugal 1975–1987
Authoritarian	None	UAE 1990–2013 Singapore 1990–2013 **Saudi Arabia 1990–2003 Bahrain 1971–2013 *Iran 1950–1979 Thailand 1961–73	*Libya 1954–1970 *Saudi Arabia 1945–1961 *Uzbekistan 2001–2005 *Pakistan 1959–69 Djibouti 2002–2013 ***Kyrgyzstan 2001–2013 *Ethiopia 1953–1977

*These nations entirely revoked U.S. access.
**U.S. decided to leave Saudi Arabia because of growing restrictions on its access.
***Kyrgyz parliament has voted to end U.S. basing rights in 2014.

The second most durable type of access has been based on shared threat with consolidated democracies. Only one country in this category has evicted U.S. forces (France in 1966). However, this result has certainly been skewed by the dynamics of the Cold War; namely the existence of a single, unifying global threat that persisted for decades. Future threats, which are likely to be shorter and contained to one region, may not yield the same result.

By contrast, the most unstable combination involves authoritarian states that enter into transactional basing agreements with the United States. In this situation, dictators who are unfettered by institutional constraints can arbitrarily threaten to evict U.S. forces unless the United States meets their terms. Consequently, the United States is forced to accept contracts that restrict its access, are of short duration, and obligate it to make increasing payments. As a result, these relationships are unpredictable, and U.S. access is always in question. Moreover, autocrats who are interested only in compensation have entirely revoked U.S. access more than any other type of regime and access relationship.[158]

Similarly, democratizing nations that are in transactional relationships with the United States usually restrict or at times even rescind U.S. access. In this situation, host nation elites foment nationalist opposition by denouncing past U.S. support for dictators and demanding that U.S. bases be removed or that access be renegotiated on more favorable terms. This anti-American

---

[158] Examples of authoritarian states that have completely rescinded U.S. access include Ethiopia (1977), Morocco (1962), Libya (1970), Saudi Arabia (1962), Uzbekistan (2005), and Pakistan (1969).

furor is partly a ploy used by elites to win popular support, but at the same time, the host government leverages this sentiment to obtain larger payments. While democratization combined with compensation-based relationships nearly always results in instability and limitations on U.S. access, it also offers an opportunity to revise the existing basing agreement so that it is more equitable and provides more stable access. For instance, Spanish President Felipe Gonzalez used the 1988 base negotiations to transform the transactional arrangement that had been negotiated by Franco into one that was founded upon shared interests. Gonzalez demanded a significant reduction in the U.S. military presence, but he also spurned a U.S. offer to pay for its continued access, thereby dispelling any sense that Spain was subordinate to the United States and creating a relationship based upon mutual respect.[159]

Alternatively, when a democratizing nation is in a shared threat relationship, it is still likely to restrict access, but at the same time more likely to want some type of U.S. military presence to remain. For example, between 2002 and 2005 the South Korean government sought to move U.S. forces away from the most populous areas as a way of mitigating the impact on local communities. In short, the South Korean governments sought to preserve the U.S. presence, because they viewed it as an important deterrent to North Korean aggression, by limiting its impact on local communities.[160] In contrast, when a democratizing state is in a transactional relationship, the incentive for greater compensation fuels rather than contains the nationalism that emerges as a part of the transition from authoritarian to democratic regimes. This is what happened in Greece in the 1980s, as discussed earlier.

Some of the combinations of regime type and access relationship have never or rarely existed. For instance, there are only two examples of consolidated democracies that had transactional relationships with the United States: Portugal (1988–1995) and Greece (1990–1998).[161] In these instances, stable democratic institutions restrained Portuguese and Greek leaders, leading them to abide by the existing basing agreements. Yet, one would also expect transactional dynamics to push the host nation to request that the agreement be renegotiated in an effort to secure larger payments.

This proved to be the case in Portugal when Prime Minister Anibal Cavaco Silva repeatedly demanded that the basing agreement be renegotiated, although he refrained from threatening to expel U.S. forces. Silva was upset because Congress, which was increasingly questioning the extensive compensation packages paid to host nations, had not authorized the level of assistance promised in the 1983 agreement.[162] The Reagan administration managed to temporarily mollify the Portuguese government by providing additional compensation in 1988, but before long Silva

---

[159] Angel Vinas, "Negotiating the U.S.-Spanish Agreements, 1953–1988: A Spanish Perspective," *Jean Monnet/Robert Schuman Paper Series*, Vol. 3, No. 7, September 2003, pp. 19–20.

[160] Yeo, 2011, pp. 122–148.

[161] Okinawa's hidden transactional model is a special case discussed in footnote 67.

[162] Clarke and O'Connor, 1993.

again petitioned the United States to renegotiate the terms of the basing agreement. By the early 1990s, however, the end of the Cold War had reduced the importance of many existing overseas facilities, and the U.S. government decided that it was not necessary to pay lavish rents for less vital legacy bases. Consequently, the 1995 basing agreement between the United States and Portugal provided only for a one-time transfer of military hardware worth $173 million.[163]

The Greek situation differed from Portugal's in one important respect: Congress allocated the amount of aid that had been promised to Greece in the 1990 Mutual Defense Cooperation Agreement.[164] Consequently, the Greek government did not have to engage in hardline bargaining tactics. Yet Greece suffered the same fate as Portugal when the United States cut base payments in the late 1990s.[165]

Similarly, the United States has never had enduring partners that were authoritarian regimes or undergoing a transition to democracy. One would expect, however, that a security consensus in an authoritarian regime would provide stability, but that it would be unlikely to persist if there were a regime change. Moreover, if the state were to democratize, one can imagine that there is a higher probability that it will experience a shift in elite beliefs that could erode the previous security consensus.

Given the complexities of combining these two variables, we used a minimum rule (taking the lowest score) to create a composite access risk metric for a number of current host nations. To identify a country's regime type, we used Freedom House's Freedom Rating, which categorizes countries as free, partly free, or not free.[166] Free corresponds with consolidated democracies, which we assign the lowest risk rating (green). Partly free represents nonconsolidated democracies or democratizing states, which we assign a moderate risk score (yellow). Not free indicates that the government is authoritarian and is given the highest risk rating (red).

For access relationship, we explored the historical record to determine the primary reason that each nation hosts U.S. forces. This qualitative assessment was necessary because there is no easily observable and quantifiable metric that can accurately identify whether an American military presence is based primarily on a shared identity, shared threat, or a transactional dynamic. In part this is due to the fact that the U.S. government does not admit that it pays for basing rights, preferring to adhere to the pretense that all of its bases overseas provide defense against common threats.[167] Because of this deliberate obfuscation, it can be difficult to correctly identify transactional basing relationships. Although the United States frequently provides

---

[163] Sandars, 2000, pp. 68–69; Cooley, 2008, pp. 168–170.

[164] The authorization of aid to Greece may be due to the influence of a Greek lobby in Congress.

[165] The Department of State notes that military assistance ended in the 1990s. U.S. Department of State, "Greece: Profile."

[166] Puddington, 2013, p. 32.

[167] Clarke and O'Connor, 1993.

significant economic and security assistance to enduring partners or countries facing a shared threat, this is not necessarily the *primary* reason that a nation provides the United States with access. Rather, the presence of economic assistance and arms sales may be due to the broader security relationship or the existence of a common threat.[168]

Because enduring partners are reliable host nations, they were given the lowest risk score (green). The mutual defense model offers a stable foundation for countering the shared threat and therefore receives a middling risk score of (yellow). Finally, transactional relationships are very unstable, so they are given a high risk score (red).

Figure 4.1 displays the scores of a select subset of countries on this composite risk metric. Not surprisingly, the United States' Western European partners—which are consolidated democracies and enduring partners—are the most reliable host nations, along with a few close Asian allies. Nevertheless, in the regions that have been identified as the highest priority—the Middle East and Southeast Asia—the United States faces greater uncertainty. In the Middle East, most of the United States' closest allies are hereditary monarchies. Given the unexpected and dramatic fashion in which many Middle Eastern dictators fell as a part of the Arab spring, it is clear that popular pressure poses a significant challenge to Middle Eastern autocrats. In Southeast Asia, the United States is on better ground because access is based upon shared threat and some of its closest partners, such as Thailand and the Philippines, are democracies—although imperfect ones.

---

[168] Harkavy, 1989, concludes that other nations provide the United States with bases in return for arms sales. This, however, is likely a spurious relationship. Pettyjohn, 2012, p. 66.

Figure 4.1. Composite Access Risk with Select Host Nations

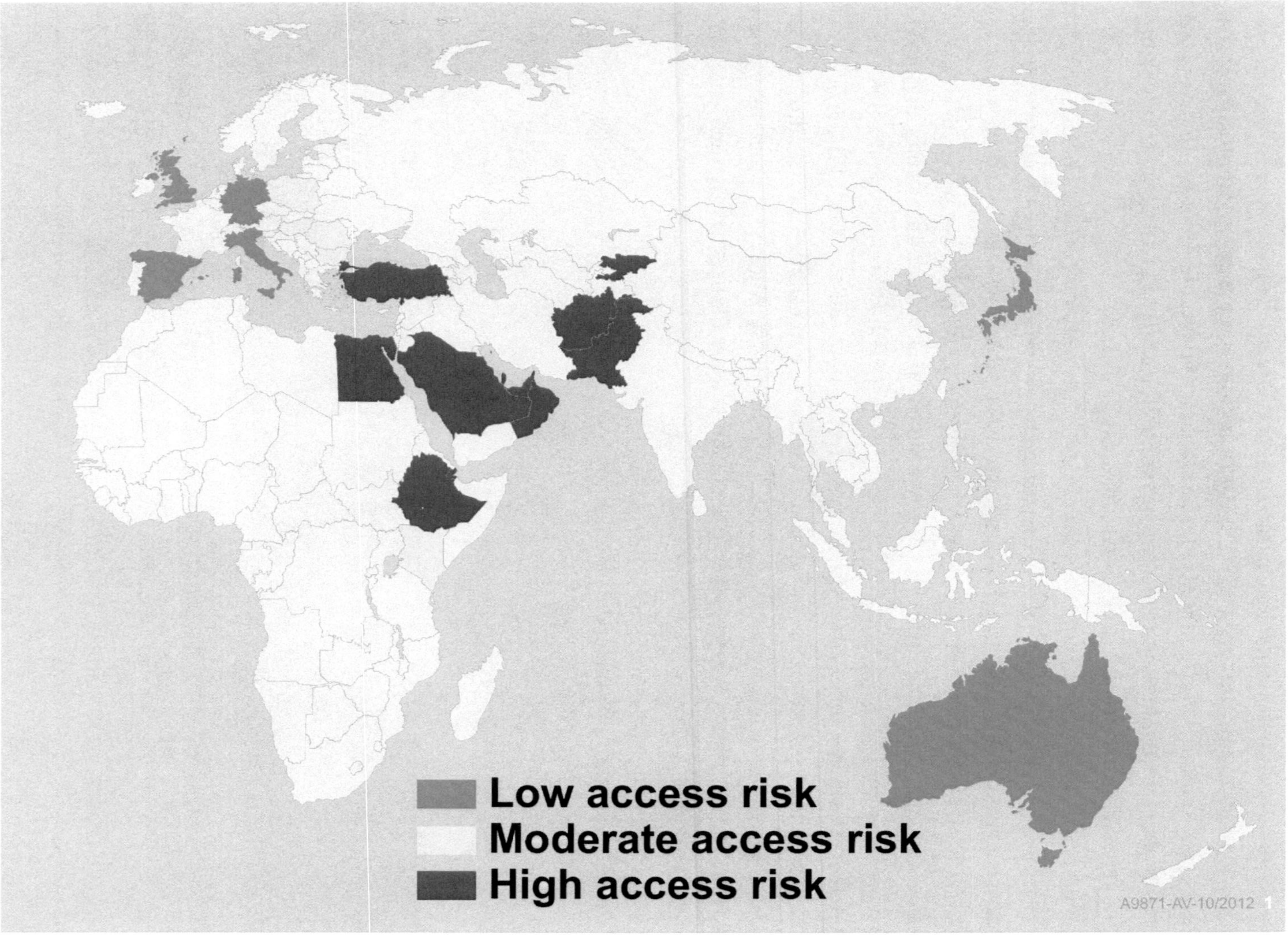

Low access risk
Moderate access risk
High access risk

A9871-AV-10/2012

Looking to the future, this methodology helps to identify potential access problems as well as locations where access is likely to be stable. For instance, Camp Lemonnier in Djibouti appears to be particularly at risk. The United States pays Djibouti an undisclosed amount for rights to its only permanent base on the African continent. Initially, this agreement was reached after President Omar Guelleh orchestrated a bidding war between the United States and France, which also uses Camp Lemonnier.[169] Moreover, there were significant protests against Guelleh's regime in 2011 and 2013.[170] Because Djibouti is an unstable authoritarian regime and transactional partner, one would expect that U.S. basing rights are going to be increasingly called into question, especially if higher rents are not forthcoming.

Similarly, Greenland, which is an autonomous province of Denmark, might be another potential trouble spot. Since the 1950s, Denmark has provided the United States with access to Thule airbase in Greenland, which today is an important radar and satellite ground station. Yet if Greenland secedes from Denmark, as the ruling Inuit Ataqatigiit Party would like, the type of access relationship could also change.[171] While Denmark is an enduring partner, Greenland is more ambivalent about the U.S. military presence. Some within Greenland would like to close the U.S. base, while others see it as a potential source of income for an otherwise impoverished nation.[172] If the United States were to pay for access to Thule, its basing rights would be less secure, as Greenland's government could use the preexisting domestic opposition as a lever to secure greater payments. At the same time, Greenland's mature democratic institutions would restrain this bargaining dynamic.

Conversely, stable democratic nations that perceive a growing shared threat are potentially reliable hosts for U.S. forces. For example, Poland, Romania, and Bulgaria, which are all consolidated democracies, have been eager to partner with the United States as a hedge against a resurgent Russia.[173] Similarly, for over a decade Georgia has sought expanded defense cooperation with the United States, but it has suffered from domestic instability. However, recent developments—in particular the October 2012 Georgian elections that led to the first peaceful transfer of power since 1991—suggest that Georgian democracy could be consolidating.[174] If Georgian democratic institutions continue to mature, Tbilisi could potentially provide U.S. forces

---

[169] In the original 2001 agreement, the United States paid Djibouti $30 million a year. Jennifer N. Brass, "Djibouti's Unusual Resource Curse," *Journal of Modern African Studies,* Vol. 46, No. 4, 2008, pp. 525–526.

[170] Abdourahim Artch, "Djibouti Police Battle Crowds Protesting Election Result," Reuters, March 1, 2013.

[171] Martin Breum and Jorgen Chemnitz, "No, Greenland Does Not Belong to China," *New York Times,* February 20, 2013.

[172] "Greenland Profile," BBC, March 12, 2013.

[173] Jim Garamone, "U.S. Establishes Full-Time Aviation Detachment in Poland," *American Forces Press Service,* November 9, 2012; Kevin Sullivan, "Romanians Eager for Long-Awaited Arrival of Yanks," *Washington Post,* February 6, 2006.

[174] Ellen Barry, "Georgia's President Concedes Defeat in Parliamentary Election," *New York Times,* October 2, 2012.

with reliable access that would give the United States greater reach into the Middle East and Central Asia, although this would almost certainly increase tensions with Russia. In general, as the United States searches for *new* basing rights, when possible, it should prioritize working with potential host nations that are stable democracies and where there is the presence of a shared threat.

In this chapter, we developed a methodology to distinguish between potentially dependable host nations and those countries that are likely to limit or abrogate U.S. basing rights. Using this approach, we identified the level of risk associated with current U.S. host nations and recommended that wherever possible the United States prioritize hosts that are stable democracies and where there is a shared threat or an enduring partnership. While this chapter examined the issue of political access, it did not speak to the complicated question of how many forces the United States needs to permanently station overseas. Chapter Five grapples with the issue of how much forward presence is required to meet U.S. national security objectives.

5. How Much Forward Presence Does the USAF Require?

In 2012, the USAF had a relatively small overseas presence, with just over 30,000 airmen stationed in Europe at seven major air bases in Germany, the UK, Turkey, Italy, and the Azores. In East Asia, the USAF had approximately 25,000 airmen stationed at six bases in South Korea, Japan, and the U.S. territory of Guam. While the USAF's post-Afghanistan presence in Central Asia has yet to be determined, it maintains a few thousand airmen at three major air bases in Qatar, the UAE, and Kuwait.[175] Yet it is unclear whether the USAF has the appropriate amount of peacetime presence overseas or whether this presence is correctly distributed to meet its alliance commitments and to deal with emerging security challenges.

This raises the question: How should the USAF think about the amount and type of overseas presence that it requires? Inevitably, numerous factors affect this decision, but there are two plausible explanations that merit further attention. First, it is often asserted that the United States' overseas presence is a legacy of the past and that stasis largely explains the number, type, and location of U.S. forces across the globe. In other words, there is a baseline level of forces the USAF typically maintains in different parts of the world. Second, it is reasonable to assume that the size of the U.S. overseas presence is driven by military contingency plans. Yet for reasons that will be discussed below, there is no convincing way to quantify peacetime force needs overseas. Therefore, rather than focusing on past levels of presence as a historical baseline or current operational plan requirements, the USAF needs to think about the balance between the purpose of its facilities, in particular where it is likely to have adequate coverage and where it is likely to see shortfalls.

Tremendous Variation in the USAF's Overseas Presence

As the USAF considers how much forward presence is needed, it can think about it through the prism of history to see how many airmen and bases it has typically had abroad. Before World War II, the United States had only a very small peacetime overseas military presence that was located primarily in U.S. territories. After the war, the United States maintained a large occupation force, but it intended to withdraw nearly all of these military personnel and abandon the bases over time.

For example, between 1945 and 1947, as the Army Air Force (AAF) demobilized, the number of airmen in Europe and the Middle East dropped precipitously, from 467,000 to 26,000.

---

[175] Major bases include Lajes (Azores), Mildenhall (UK), Lakenheath (UK), Spangdahlem (Germany), Ramstein (Germany), Aviano (Italy), Incirlik (Turkey), Osan (ROK), Kunsan (ROK), Misawa (Japan), Yokota (Japan), Kadena (Japan), Andersen (Guam), Ali Al Salem (Kuwait), Al-Udeid (Qatar), and Al-Dhafra (UAE). Exact personnel numbers for South Korea and the Persian Gulf are not reported (Defense Manpower Data Center, 2010).

At the same time, the AAF withdrew all but 43,000 of the 445,000 airmen that had been stationed in Asia.[176] Consequently, by 1947 U.S. Air Forces in Europe (USAFE) consisted of only 13 airbases (nearly all of which were in West Germany). Airbases were needed to support the occupation, but the number was expected to decline, as USAFE planned to remove all of its combat aircraft from the continent.[177] In mid-1948, then Vice Chief of Staff General Hoyt Vandenberg described USAFE as a "token" force of only 19,000 airmen.[178] By contrast, 45,000 airmen remained in Asia to occupy Japan and to defend U.S. territories. As tensions with the Soviet Union mounted, Strategic Air Command bombers began rotations to Germany and the United Kingdom. Moreover, during the Soviet Union's blockade of Berlin between 1948 and 1949, the USAF temporary deployed additional combat units to Europe and Asia.

Despite these early developments, the onset of the Korean War was the catalyst that precipitated the establishment of a large peacetime U.S. military presence abroad. As a result of this pivotal event, U.S. defense budgets grew prodigiously, and many partner nations were so fearful of communist aggression that they granted the United States indefinite basing rights.[179] Consequently, between June 1950 and 1953 the number of airmen overseas nearly tripled.[180] The regions that experienced the greatest expansion of USAF presence were in Northeast Asia and in Western Europe. By 1953, the USAF presence in East Asia consisted of 130,546 airmen at 28 major air bases, with most of the growth occurring in South Korea, where the USAF had essentially no presence before 1950, and in Japan, where the number of airmen more than doubled.[181] At the same time, the USAF presence in Europe had exploded to 107,037 airmen stationed at 42 major bases, which were primarily located in West Germany, France, and the UK.[182]

Although Europe and Asia hosted the vast majority of the USAF's overseas forces, the Korean War prompted the development of air bases around the world. In North Africa and the Middle East, for example, the number of USAF forces grew dramatically at Wheelus AB in

---

[176] Thomas Sturm, *USAF Overseas Forces and Bases: 1947–1967*, Washington, D.C.: Office of Air Force History, 1969, p. 2.

[177] The other locations were one base each in Austria, Libya, and Liberia. All bases were used to support the occupation forces. Lawrence R. Benson, *USAF Aircraft Basing in Europe, North Africa, and the Middle East, 1945–1980*, Ramstein Air Base, Germany: Office of History, Headquarters United States Air Forces in Europe, 1981, Declassified on July 20, 2011, p. 9.

[178] Quoted in Sturm, 1969, p. 4–5.

[179] Pettyjohn, 2012.

[180] Personnel numbers from this point forward were taken from Defense Manpower Data Center (2010), while the number of bases was compiled from multiple sources.

[181] Major bases include only operating airfields that host USAF aircraft. Between 1950 and 1953, the USAF presence expanded from 30,663 airmen to 70,817 in Japan, and from a single airman to 44,650 in South Korea.

[182] Between 1950 and 1953, the USAF presence expanded from 17,845 to 37,833 in West Germany, from 4,391 to 42,272 in the UK, and from 169 to 17,308 in France.

Libya, Dhahran Airfield in Saudi Arabia, and the several airbases built for Strategic Air Command operations in Morocco.[183]

The USAF's force posture in Europe continued to grow and peaked in 1957 at 119,247 airman at 49 major air bases. By contrast, because the 1953 armistice stabilized the situation on the Korean peninsula, there was a rapid drawdown of combat forces in South Korea. Most of these units were relocated to Japan or the United States, and the USAF presence on the peninsula was consolidated at a few remaining air bases. Consequently, by 1957 there were only 78,967 airmen and 21 major air bases in East Asia. (See Figures 5.1 and 5.2.)

Figure 5.1. Major USAF Bases Overseas, 1953–2011

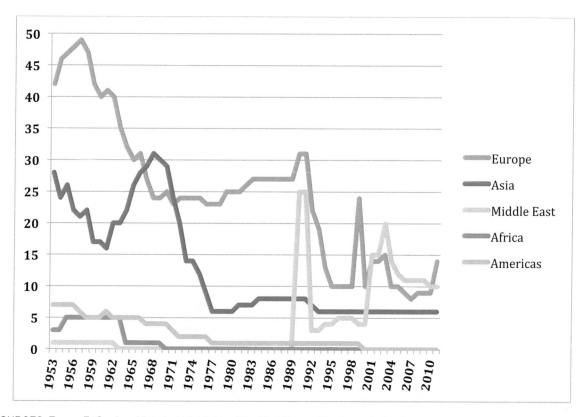

SOURCES: Tomas F. Gordon, *Historical Highlights of the First Twenty-Five Years of PACAF*, 1957–1981, Hickam Air Force Base, Hawaii: Office of History Pacific Air Forces, July 30, 1982; Thomas S. Snyder and Daniel F. Harrington, *Historical Highlights United States Air Forces in Europe 1942–1997*, Ramstein Air Base, Germany: USAFE Office of History, March 14, 1997; U.S. Air Force, *United States Air Force Statistical Digest*, Washington, D.C.: Headquarters Air Force, multiple years; and GlobalSecurity.org.

---

[183] These Moroccan bases were used for Strategic Air Command operations, as was Dhahran. But Dhahran also supported military air transport system operations, while Wheelus Field was an important USAFE training range. Sturm, 1969 pp. 18–20. Between 1950 and 1953, the USAF presence expanded from 468 to 1,003 in Saudi Arabia, from nine to 8,828 in Morocco, and from 940 to 5,366 in Libya. Nationalist pressure led to the expulsion of USAF forces from all three countries during the 1960s.

Figure 5.2. Active Duty Airmen Deployed Overseas, 1953–2011

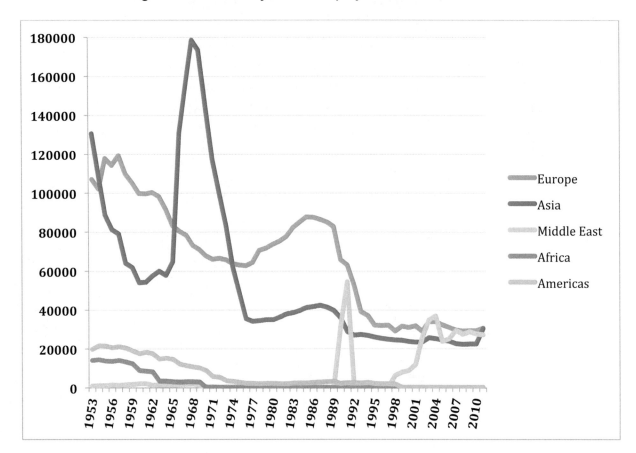

SOURCE: Defense Manpower Data Center, 2010.

As the nation faced a growing balance of payments crisis in the late 1950s, the Eisenhower administration canceled existing plans to further increase the U.S. overseas military presence and instead demanded reductions in the current global posture. These cuts, however, were disproportionally borne by the Pacific Air Forces (PACAF), which experienced a 49 percent reduction in total facilities between 1958 and 1961.[184] Nevertheless, the USAF posture in Europe, North Africa, and the Middle East also declined, although these reductions were due to a number of factors, including developments in technology that reduced—although did not eliminate— Strategic Air Command's reliance on forward bases, and rising nationalism that resulted in the expulsion of U.S. forces.

The Kennedy administration also sought to improve the nation's finances by eliminating nonessential military operations at home and abroad; however, this effort was overshadowed by the United States' deepening involvement in Southeast Asia. In 1962, the USAF had less than 60,000 airmen in Asia at 21 major airbases, but as a result of the war in Vietnam that number had ballooned by 1968 to over 178,000 airmen at 31 major airbases in Taiwan, South Vietnam,

---

[184] Sturm, p. 34. Total facilities includes all types of installations and not just airfields.

Thailand, the Philippines, Japan, Guam, and South Korea. At the same time, the Vietnam War diverted resources from the European theater, so that by 1975 the USAFE presence had dropped to 63,176 airmen at 24 air bases. As the United States withdrew from Vietnam, it voluntarily relinquished many airbases in Southeast Asia that were no longer needed, but it had hoped to maintain a small USAF presence in Thailand. Because the Thai government had been offended by the high-handed U.S. behavior during the *Mayaguez* crisis, it took a hardline during base negotiations, resulting in the termination of U.S. bases rights in 1975.[185] Consequently, by 1977 the USAF was left with only six major airbases in Asia and 34,141 airmen. In response to the expanded Soviet military presence in the region, the number of airmen again exceeded 40,000 in the mid-1980s. The next significant change—another reduction in PACAF's force posture— coincided with, but was not caused by, the end of the Cold War. Instead, this was an involuntary contraction that was brought about when the Philippines decided to oust U.S. forces. The eruption of Mount Pinatubo forced the USAF to withdraw preemptively in 1991 before the final decision to terminate U.S. bases rights had been made. Since that time, the USAF presence has been concentrated in Northeast Asia with, somewhere between 7,000 and 9,000 airmen in South Korea and 12,000 to 15,000 airmen in Japan.

In the 1980s, the Reagan administration's military buildup slightly expanded USAFE, so that by 1985 there were more than 87,000 airmen at 27 major air bases. However, as tensions with the Soviet Union abated in the late 1980s, the USAF presence in Europe was voluntarily drawn down in an effort to yield a peace dividend. Between 1988 and 1994, the number of airmen declined by 45 percent, and the number of airbases was cut nearly in half, leaving only 37,211 airmen and 13 airbases in Europe. In the past decade, there have been additional fluctuations in USAFE's force posture, resulting from contingency operations in Kosovo, Afghanistan, Iraq, and Libya.

While the USAF presence in Asia and Europe has significantly declined from its Cold War peaks, the USAF force posture has grown considerably in the Middle East. Throughout the Cold War, the USAF had a very small presence in the Middle East, consisting of one major airbase at Dhahran airfield in Saudi Arabia. But in 1962, pressure from Pan-Arabist forces impelled King Saud to not renew the United States' basing rights. There was no significant USAF presence in the region until Saddam Hussein invaded Kuwait in 1990, precipitating the deployment of more than 54,000 airmen to 25 major air bases in 1991. Yet soon after Operation Desert Storm ended, the USAF withdrew most of its forces, leaving only a small residual force of a few hundred airmen at several airbases in the Persian Gulf to enforce the no-fly zone over Southern Iraq. As Saddam increasingly defied United Nations inspectors and challenged the international sanctions against his regime, the USAF presence grew, so that by 1999 there were more than 8,000 airmen at four major air bases. The September 11, 2001, attacks against the United States and the

---

[185] R. Sean Randolph, *The United States and Thailand: Alliance Dynamics, 1950–1985*, Berkley, Calif.: Institute of East Asian Studies, University of California, 1986, p. 192.

subsequent operations against Afghanistan precipitated another surge into the Middle East, so that by 2002 there were nearly 26,000 airmen at 15 major air bases in the Middle East. The USAF presence expanded further with the launch of OIF in 2003, but has since declined: In 2011, there were over 27,000 airmen at 10 major air bases in the region.

Several observations can be made about this historical analysis. First, while Europe and Asia were initially outliers that contained the vast majority of the USAF's overseas presence, by 2011 there was rough parity between East Asia, the Middle East, and Europe.[186] Second, and most importantly, these quantitative metrics reveal that aggregate presence levels have fluctuated dramatically in response to changing strategic circumstances, especially periods of escalating and declining threat. Moreover, because there has been tremendous variation over time and across regions, these metrics are not very useful for understanding how much forward presence the USAF requires. Ultimately, there is no baseline level of overseas presence that the USAF can identify as what it has maintained in a particular region and therefore use to guide what is needed in the future.

Military Requirements and Forward Presence

Because the past yields few insights into how much presence the USAF requires, one could instead focus on the present, in particular military requirements for current contingency plans. Yet rigidly adhering to current operational plans does not give the United States the flexibility to meet future security challenges, which are often uncertain. More importantly, the relationship between operational plans and posture rests on a flawed and circular logic. Because of the stasis associated with force posture, peacetime presence is an *input* to rather than an *output* of the contingency planning process. In short, operational plans are used to justify forward presence, but forward presence is a constant that shapes the operational plans.

The historical discussion above makes clear that when viewed at the regional level, the number of personnel deployed abroad and the number of U.S. bases are overwhelmingly determined by periods of escalating and declining threat. It is also apparent that the number of U.S. forces abroad during peacetime is insufficient to meet the demands of major contingencies. Nevertheless, at the regional level it seems plausible that operational requirements determine the number of forces that are stationed abroad during peacetime.

This is a reasonable assumption, since U.S. military planning involves multiple, complex, and highly detailed "requirements" processes. In these processes, there is a widely held expectation that the location, size, and characteristics of forces permanently deployed overseas are the direct and immediate product of a formal and recent process. For example, in the theater campaign planning process, combatant commands (COCOMs) conduct an annual assessment of their posture needs. In this process, regional COCOMs compare theater campaign plan (TCP)

---

[186] 30,439 airmen at six bases in Asia; 30,779 at 14 bases in Europe; 27,218 at 10 bases in the Middle East.

requirements with existing capabilities, identifying gaps and risks. They are then supposed to propose changes to the posture plan to address any shortcomings that were discovered. These findings are documented in the posture annex to the annual TCP.[187] Thus, in this process (see Figure 5.3), the number, type, and location of forward-based forces are supposed to be determined by the TCP requirements. In short, force posture is believed to be an output of the military planning process.

Figure 5.3. Common View That Force Posture Is an Output of the Requirements Process

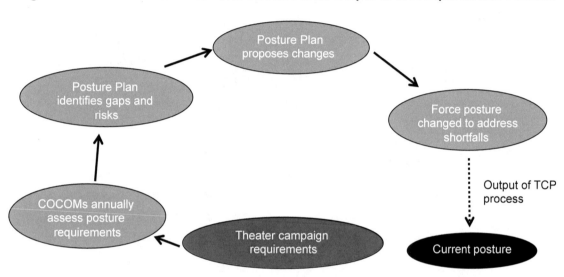

Yet we know that most U.S. forces permanently based abroad are located at bases that date back to World War II or the Korean War and that unit configurations (e.g., how many squadrons of what type aircraft are located at a particular base) change very slowly, typically over many years or decades.[188] We noted earlier in this report that global posture is resistant to change, either quantitatively or qualitatively. Modifying an existing overseas presence or creating a new one is usually a very complex and time-consuming process that requires negotiations with the host nation, persuading Congress to appropriate the funds for military construction or relocation, and, in the event of closures, remediating any environmental damage. This reality suggests that force posture, at least writ large, is better characterized as a near-term constant rather than a variable that military planners can manipulate. Figure 5.4 illustrates this alternative perspective that sees current posture as a constraint or input to planning.

---

[187] Joint Staff, "Global Defense Posture," unpublished background paper, April 16, 2012.

[188] For example, the 18th Wing has been based at Kadena AB, Japan, since 1954 and has been flying F-15 fighters since 1979. See 18th Wing History.

Figure 5.4. Forces Deployed Abroad Are an Input to, Not an Output of, the Requirements Process

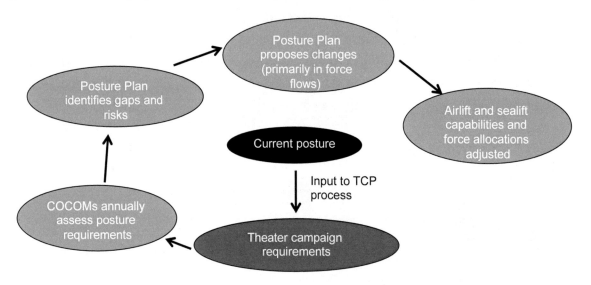

Staff officers working on military plans know that the peacetime TCP requirements process has little chance of triggering major changes in posture over the near term. Forces that are permanently based abroad are, therefore, treated as *inputs* to the planning process rather than *outputs*. Rather, the focus for planners working near-term plans is to ensure that U.S. forces at home and in other theaters are allocated to their priority plans and that sufficient air- and sealift is available to support the crisis or contingency deployment of those forces. This is both because the bulk of U.S. combat power is based on U.S. territory rather than abroad and because assigning forces to plans is exponentially easier than moving forces to or among overseas bases. This does not mean that forces permanently based abroad do not have important, perhaps vital, roles to play in various contingencies, but the forces are given these roles because they are already in the theater; they were not put in the theater to meet these specific military needs.

The Posture Triangle and Peacetime Presence Needs

Given the problems associated with the above approaches to identifying USAF presence needs, this is where a consistent and logical framework—such as the posture triangle—can be useful. Examining the posture triangle, and in particular how it is evolving, provides useful insights into how the USAF should think about presence, what type of presence is required, and how much presence is needed.

The posture triangle illustrates how access to foreign soil is necessary to tie the United States to critical partners and regions, create and sustain military effects, and enable the projection of power worldwide. In the past, many USAF bases simultaneously served many or even all of these functions. Recent trends suggest that the roles of overseas bases are changing. On the one hand, some strategic anchors continue to also serve as important support links. For example, Ramstein AB, as a Tier I AMC en route location, is a vital support link. Along with U.S.

European Command and other military headquarters, Army combat brigades, and other USAF activities, Ramstein helps underpin the U.S. security relationship with Germany. In the Asia-Pacific, Yokota AB, on the Japanese island of Honshu, plays a similarly critical role in the en route infrastructure and, along with the carrier strike group homeported at Yokosuka, major USMC bases, and other USAF bases and headquarters, is part of the strategic anchor tying Washington to Tokyo. Nevertheless, it is also worth noting that the vast majority of AMC en route locations require a relatively small permanent presence and that there are only a handful of these top-tier AMC locations worldwide.

On the other hand, as one looks forward, a divide appears to be emerging between strategic anchors and FOLs. As a consequence, emerging and future strategic anchors are likely to be quite different from what existed in the past. In Europe, for example, the USAF's existing strategic anchors are well positioned to serve as FOLs in European contingencies, but fighter forces would have to deploy forward to conduct sustained operations in Africa or the Middle East. Conversely, the USAF strategic anchors in Asia are well positioned to deal with contingencies in Northeast Asia, but emerging long-range precision-strike systems—in particular tactical ballistic missiles—will limit their ability to function as FOLs. Moreover, most of the strategic anchors in Japan and South Korea are too far north to be useful as FOLs for Southeast Asian contingencies. The Middle East is the one region where strategic anchors and FOLs continue to have the greatest overlap; however, this could change in the future if Iran deploys a larger and more accurate missile force (limiting the potential usefulness of some bases as FOLs) and operations in Afghanistan come to an end (limiting the need for some bases to act as FOLs). Given that force posture tends to persist, it is absolutely essential that the USAF take these long-term trends into account.

Finally, future strategic anchors will not necessarily be FOLs, because partner nations might want only a small symbolic U.S. commitment and not tolerate a large permanent U.S. military presence in peacetime. Future strategic anchors, therefore, are not likely to be large U.S. bases, as they were during the Cold War. Because the Cold War was a long-term competition with defined front lines, the strategic anchors established during the 1950s and 1960s were characterized by a large, permanent, U.S. military presence, largely consisting of major combat units (e.g. divisions, fighter wings, carrier battle groups) as well as military dependents.

Today, strategic anchors are evolving and as a result increasingly stand in contrast to the sprawling American communities that were established overseas during the Cold War. While long-standing allies are willing to maintain legacy bases, few prospective partners desire a large U.S. military presence. Three trends—rising nationalism (and the concomitant resentment towards U.S. troops' extraterritorial rights), the increasingly free flow of information, and the expanding influence of public opinion on foreign policy—have made nations reluctant to host U.S. main operating bases. Because of this growing sensitivity to any foreign military presence, the strategic anchor of the future is likely to be composed of smaller units tailored to the particular needs of that partner (e.g., missile defense). Moreover, new strategic anchors are likely to rely more on rotational forces, consisting of a relatively small permanent presence and fewer accompanied tours. Finally, strategic anchors are likely to shift from being exclusively American bases to joint facilities that are shared with host nation forces.

As the USAF rethinks its global posture, it should consider whether past metrics—the number of airmen and bases that it has overseas—are the most relevant. Our framework suggests that a more salient focus is whether the USAF has sufficient capacity for each of the three purposes for which it requires access to foreign bases. In other words, the USAF should focus on the balance among strategic anchors, FOLs, and support links and on identifying where it has adequate numbers and where there are shortfalls.

As discussed above, the USAF has a significant presence in 8 of the 13 strategic anchor countries. Most of these are enduring partners who strongly desire a continuing permanent U.S. military presence. Since, along with carrier strike groups and USMC/U.S. Army brigades, a USAF wing is widely recognized as a concrete symbol of U.S. commitment and capability, the USAF should expect a continuing demand for wing headquarters and subordinate units in many top-tier strategic anchor countries. While in some cases a larger permanent presence may be called for, other partners (e.g., Australia) prefer a smaller footprint. Consequently, the USAF should be prepared to provide rotational forces at the squadron level to support a new model of strategic anchor, such as may be found in Singapore and, perhaps, the Philippines.

The USAF also has a robust global transportation infrastructure, which it needs to preserve but not necessarily expand. This en route infrastructure is absolutely critical, but it may be near its optimal level. In contrast, due to the changing nature of strategic anchors—which are increasingly inadequately located, too vulnerable, or too small to serve as FOLs—the USAF needs to develop additional FOLs.

As the USAF adapts its posture to deal with future security challenges, it should keep in mind that there is not one simple overarching rule for determining the appropriate size for its overseas presence. Instead it is essential that the USAF in particular, and the United States more generally, take into account the specific domestic and international context each host nation faces and tailor its presence to fit these circumstances. Moreover, given the changing nature of USAF's posture and the existing posture that it has in place, having sufficient infrastructure in place to support operations has become more important than the aggregate number of forces overseas.

6. Findings and Recommendations

This study set out to answer fundamental questions about USAF force posture: Why does the USAF need a global posture? Where does it need access? What types of partners offer the most reliable peacetime access? How much forward presence does the USAF require? To answer these questions, we pursued several lines of research. First, we developed a logical framework, the posture triangle, to link U.S. national security requirements to specific types of posture. Second, we assessed the utility of dozens of airfields to meet mission demands for nine diverse scenarios. Third, we integrated our results with analysis conducted in previous (FY11) research for the USAF—which together cover almost 30 scenarios and over 600 airfields. Fourth, we developed a method to assess peacetime access risk. Finally, we used the posture triangle framework to offer insights on sizing USAF overseas forces. Our research findings are presented below.

Why Does the USAF Need a Global Posture?

Although it is true that U.S. geography and overseas territories convey significant military advantages, they alone are insufficient to meet three critical U.S. security requirements: (1) maintain security ties to close partners and key regions, (2) conduct effective operations, and (3) sustain global military activities. For the first requirement, since the end of World War II the United States has relied on some type of enduring military presence to maintain these ties. Although this presence will evolve and at times may be modest in size, there is a world of difference between an enduring presence and none. Returning U.S. forces home may be attractive in theory, however, U.S. experience since World War II confirms that it is extremely difficult to accomplish reassurance, deterrence, and regional stability missions with forces based exclusively in the United States.

Regarding the second national security requirement, U.S. territory alone is insufficient to conduct sustained operations outside of the western hemisphere, whether for disaster relief or combat. Access to foreign territory is needed to generate operational effects. This is true for the Army, the Marine Corps, the Navy, and the Air Force. With respect to USAF force structure, current aircraft designs lack the range and speed to conduct sustained global round-trip missions from U.S. territory alone. Even long-range bombers are dependent on aerial refueling for many missions, and there are significant limits to air refueling support conducted exclusively from U.S. soil.[189] Future technological breakthroughs may change this conclusion, but aircraft expected to

---

[189] During Operations Desert Storm, Desert Strike, Allied Force, Iraqi Freedom, and Odyssey Dawn, bombers did conduct round-trip missions from the continental United States, but all benefited from tanker support launched from overseas bases.

dominate USAF force structure over the next 20 to 30 years are highly dependent (either directly or indirectly) on access to forward facilities.

Finally, access to foreign territory is necessary to host support links. The links—en route airfields, ports, logistics facilities, and communications and early warning sites—are all constrained by either the range and endurance of the forces they support or other geographically driven factors (e.g., for early warning radars).

Where Does the USAF Need Basing and Access?

Our analysis, which considered ongoing activities and operations, key relationships, and the demands of almost 30 diverse scenarios, identified 13 strategic anchor countries (see Figure 3.1), 11 basing clusters (see Figure 3.5), and 35 en route airfields (see Table 3.3) as particularly valuable. Depending on how USAF senior leaders choose to weight the probability and importance of the scenarios, the demand for basing and access could be somewhat higher or lower than these numbers.

If we do some modest rounding, this analysis suggests a rough rule of thumb for planners: 12-12-36. That is, as the USAF plans for future demands on the force, it should expect to be called upon to maintain forces and facilities in roughly a dozen strategic anchor countries, to have the capacity to conduct operations from FOLs in roughly a dozen basing clusters, and to require en route airfields in about three dozen locations.[190] Although this may sound like a large posture, the USAF peacetime presence at most of the en route locations is minimal, and there is no peacetime presence at most FOLs. Also, the specific demands on the USAF at these locations vary greatly.

For example, where another service is not meeting U.S. strategic anchor needs, the USAF might deploy fighter aircraft, tankers, ISR platforms, other capabilities, or a composite organization combining all these elements. FOL demands vary across missions and platforms. They may be met in some cases by existing airfields, whereas in others U.S. and partner nations may need to make selected investments in operating surfaces, parking, fuel systems, or other infrastructure. Finally, although the USAF requires a few high-capacity mobility hubs, such as Ramstein AB, the majority of locations in the current air mobility en route system place quite modest demands on USAF resources because they either have no permanent staffs or the staffs are quite small. Additionally, most of these airfields are not owned or maintained by the USAF. They are either commercial, sister service, or partner nation airfields. This is a great bargain when the small investment in personnel is compared with the operational versatility and resilience that is gained from regular access to these facilities.

---

[190] This is somewhat smaller than the 2025 en route system found in AMC's 2010 white paper.

What Types of Security Partnerships Minimize Peacetime Access Risk?

This study developed an access risk metric based on regime type and the nature of basing relationship. Domestic political institutions play a large role in a host nation's propensity to contest U.S. bases and access, with consolidated democracies the most dependable, nonconsolidated democracies less reliable, and authoritarian regimes the most problematic. We use Freedom House scores (free, partly free, not free) to rate host nations on this metric. Although regime type influences the reliability of peacetime access, other factors, including differing ideational motivations, strategic perspectives, and bargaining incentives, are key to understanding access risk.

We argue that a second variable—the type of access relationship—captures these different factors and significantly impacts the level of risk. Access relationships fall into one of three categories: a desire for material benefits (transactional), a shared perception of threat (mutual defense), or a deep security consensus (enduring partnership). In the transactional model, the host government makes bases on its territory available to secure material benefits in the form of rents, economic assistance, or arms sales. Compensation-driven access creates an unstable dynamic, because the host nation has every incentive to highlight problems associated with the U.S. presence to extract larger payments. A mutual defense relationship, in contrast, is built on a shared threat perception. This is a stable foundation for cooperation as long as the U.S. presence remains focused on countering the mutual security challenge. This is the most frequent reason nations give the United States access. In this relationship, however, the United States is likely to encounter difficulties if it tries to use its bases or forces for purposes unrelated to the mutual threat. The most stable relationship is the enduring partnership. The countries in this category all initially granted the United States basing rights for a reason (either shared threat or compensation) that has since disappeared. Yet, these nations continue host U.S. forces because of an elite security consensus that the U.S. military plays a stabilizing role in the world and that the host countries have broad shared interests that are advanced by hosting U.S. forces.

We found that regime type and access relationship interact with one another and that particular combinations are especially stable or volatile. For instance, to date all of the United States' enduring partners have been consolidated democracies. Well-entrenched democratic institutions make it difficult for governments to modify or abandon existing basing agreements, while the shared identity fostered by a common form of government embeds U.S. access in a broader set of security cooperation activities. The second most durable type of access is based on a shared threat with consolidated democracies. Only one country in this category (France, 1966) evicted U.S. forces, although the nature of post–Cold War relationships may make this somewhat more common in the future. By contrast, the least stable combinations involve authoritarian states that enter into transactional relationships with the United States. In this situation, dictators who are unfettered by institutional constraints can arbitrarily threaten to evict U.S. forces unless their terms are met. As a result, these relationships are unpredictable, and access is always in question. Autocrats who are only interested in compensation have entirely revoked U.S. access more than any other type of regime and access relationship.

How Much Forward Presence Does the United States Require?

It is much easier to identify the benefits of forward presence, both political and military, than to quantify how large a force is required to meet national security objectives. Deterrence, reassurance, and regional stability objectives are strongly tied to perceptions of U.S. capabilities and will. U.S. capability and will are both demonstrated through the forward deployment of forces that possess relevant capabilities in numbers that are generally recognized as significant. For example, a USN carrier strike group, a Marine Corps expeditionary brigade, a U.S. Army brigade combat team, or a USAF wing are all widely recognized as significant combat formations and proof of a serious U.S. commitment to the partner. Where threats are more limited, smaller deployments (e.g., a Patriot air defense battery or battalion) may meet such needs. That said, there is no authoritative means to show how variations in force size (e.g., adding or subtracting a few fighter squadrons) enhance or detract from these higher-level goals.

In contrast, theater campaign plan requirements are readily quantified, and the effects of force size changes can be shown in theater combat simulations. Although this may appear to offer a means to size forward forces, in practice it is problematic. Because DoD and the military services use multiple "requirements" processes in force planning, there is a common perception that the type and size of permanently deployed forward forces is the product of such a process. This isn't the case. TCP requirements change much more often than force posture does. Force posture is extremely resistant to change, due to the complex interplay of three factors: the U.S. planning, programming, and budgeting process; domestic political dynamics in both the United States and host country; and the intricacies of negotiations between sovereign nations. Major changes (whether expansion or shrinkage) in the type, size, and location of foreign forces have strategic implications for the host nation: Enhancements may be viewed as provocative by some constituencies, while reductions may be seen by others as undermining deterrence. Major force changes also raise a host of local concerns about land use, safety, noise, economic, and social impacts. For these reasons, permanent force changes are usually relatively small, with large changes occurring only rarely. Given this reality, theater campaign planners can successfully make the case to retain forward forces because of their value but rarely can initiate major changes. Thus, forward force size is typically an input to rather than an output of this process. To the extent that the TCP identifies additional force requirements, they would be deployed during a crisis period from the United States or other regions.

So how should the U.S. size forward forces? We suggest a multifaceted approach. First, where current forward forces can be shown as vital in meeting TCP requirements they should be left in place. Second, where enduring partners show a strong desire to maintain current forces, DoD should seek to maintain a concrete symbol of U.S. commitment and capability, such as a

Marine Corps or Army brigade, Navy carrier strike group, or USAF wing. The long-term benefits from these relationships greatly exceed the costs of maintaining some level of presence in key partner nations. In these cases, the United States and the host nation should work together to evolve the forces and facilities in ways that are cost-effective in meeting both nations' security objectives. The USAF should expect a continuing demand for USAF wings in many strategic anchor countries. In some cases, a larger permanent presence will be called for; other partners (e.g., Australia) will prefer a smaller footprint. Third, DoD combatant commands and the services should explicitly embrace a capabilities-based approach in determining the size of forward forces. This approach would seek to identify key operational metrics that could be used to determine the type and size of forces desired in a given region. In some cases (e.g., U.S. European Command and U.S. Africa Command), forces based in one command might be the primary force provider for another.

Recommendations

Use an Integrated Framework to Explain Global Posture

There are many potential explanations for the erosion of American elite support for an extensive overseas military presence. The end of the Cold War, a desire to be done with major military operations in Southwest Asia, fiscal concerns, and resentment toward some partners for not contributing more to their own defense all may be factors. It also appears that U.S. government explanations for global posture are not resonating with core audiences, whether in Congress or among American opinion leaders. For example, DoD's January 2012 strategic guidance[191] offers a thoughtful explanation of U.S. strategy and a regionally based rationale for changes in posture, but it does not offer readers an integrated framework to understand global posture more broadly. Such a framework should explicitly demonstrate how specific elements of posture are needed to meet specific national security goals. We developed the posture triangle as a framework that can incorporate both qualitative and quantitative inputs and answer fundamental posture questions, ranging from "Why are we abroad?" to "How many bases are required?" The framework is intended to be a useful tool for both internal DoD planning and for public outreach. The framework can be used to think through posture needs in a wide range of settings and is more accessible to a wider audience, most of whom are not regional or country specialists attuned to the types of arguments typically made in DoD strategy documents. We recommend that DoD and the USAF either incorporate this framework into future posture documents and processes or develop their own approach. Either way, global posture needs to be explained and justified within a framework that goes beyond arguments that are peculiar to a given country or region.

---

[191] Department of Defense, *Sustaining U.S. Global Leadership: Priorities for 21st Century Defense*, Washington, D.C., January 2012.

Maintain Strategic Anchor Locations in Key Regions and with Enduring Partners

The fundamental purpose of U.S. national security strategy is to protect American interests without having to resort to bloody and costly armed conflict. To accomplish this, U.S. planners focus on measures to enhance regional stability, deterrence of potential foes, and reassurance of partners and allies. Maintaining an enduring military presence in key regions is widely viewed as having contributed substantially to these goals. The size and type of presence should be tailored to the particular needs of the host nation and United States and may include one, some, or all U.S. services. In many cases, the permanent presence may be quite small, and in all cases rotational forces can (and do) supplement those permanently deployed abroad.

We identify the United Kingdom, Germany, Italy, Spain, Japan, Korea, and Australia as top-tier strategic anchors—countries that have hosted permanent and often large U.S. facilities for 50 or more years. Kuwait, Bahrain, Qatar, and the UAE are strategic anchor locations in the Persian Gulf and key partners in regional stability efforts. In Southeast Asia, Singapore has long hosted key USN logistics facilities and is now hosting USN littoral combat ships on rotational deployments. Finally, the Philippines, a Cold War–era strategic anchor for the United States, may once again play that role if current negotiations produce a new agreement that expands U.S. access to ports and airfields.

Expand Access to Potential Forward Operating Locations in Key Regions

During the Cold War, USAF bases, such as Ramstein AB in Germany and Kadena AB in Japan, played dual roles as strategic anchors and FOLs. Today, we see FOL and strategic anchor needs diverging, for two reasons. First, emerging long-range precision-strike capabilities in countries such as China and Iran will increasingly constrain use of the most forward bases as FOLs. Many bases that play vital roles as strategic anchors during peacetime may be limited in effectiveness during some phases of conflicts. This suggests a growing role for dispersal base FOLs to, at minimum, supplement forward bases during the most intense phases of combat. Second, existing strategic anchor locations are too few in number and/or too geographically concentrated to meet all U.S. needs for FOLs. For example, none of the strategic anchors is in Africa. To better prepare the USAF for potential operations across a wide range of scenarios, we recommend working with partner nations to identify and selectively develop FOLs in 11 "basing clusters" (see Figure 3.5). Most of these would have no enduring U.S. presence. Periodic small training visits or exercises with the host nation would typify the U.S. presence.

Use Basing Clusters to Minimize Access Risk

As noted above, the highest risk to peacetime access occurs when dictators provide access exclusively to receive compensation. These arrangements should be avoided except in extreme situations. That said, any purely transactional relationship (whatever the regime type) or access agreement with an authoritarian regime (even if mutual defense) is almost as risky. For this reason, U.S. planners should seek a cluster of bases in those regions where they have no alternatives but to accept these riskier access arrangements. As discussed in Chapter Three, the cluster idea identifies multiple reasonably proximate airfields that offer similar operational benefits and seeks to develop several. For example, although USAF operational needs might not require a continuation of current access arrangements in Kuwait, Bahrain, Qatar, the UAE, and Oman in the future, it would be prudent to maintain access in several for every one that is operationally vital. Likewise, U.S. policymakers should avoid publicly describing any particular facility or country as indispensable. Appropriate deference and appreciation can be paid to overseas partners without giving them undue power in facility access negotiations. Finally, basing clusters have the additional benefit of increasing operational resilience in the face of direct military threats to any of these airfields.

Expand USAF Capability to Support Rotational Forces

Rotational forces have multiple benefits. Continuous rotational forces have proven to be an effective alternative in locations where a permanent U.S. presence is not politically viable. Periodic rotational forces are often used to supplement forward forces and to expand the range of capabilities available to theater commands, as seen in the regular rotation of USAF F-22s through Kadena AB in Japan. Since permanent force posture is difficult and slow to change (either up or down), rotational forces offer policymakers and commanders an agile policy instrument that can be used to support multiple policy objectives, including deterrent signaling and reassurance of partners.

Rotational forces are also attractive to many partner nations because they offer many of the benefits of a permanent force without the large footprint and domestic political complications. In addition to continuous rotational forces deployed for several decades to key Southwest Asia locations, the USN's new littoral combat ship is now deployed to Singapore on a rotational basis, and in 2012 the USMC began rotating forces through Darwin, Australia.

Although the USAF has decades of successful experience with both types of rotational forces and developed the Air Expeditionary Force construct to support such deployments, airmen are quick to note that force rotations are not without problems (cost, lost training opportunities, and personnel impacts in particular) and that current demand may already be unsustainable. Above all, it is much more costly to rotate forces than to permanently base them abroad. In cases where a continuous presence is necessary, permanent basing will always be more cost-effective. Thus, continuous rotations should be minimized to the extent possible, recognizing that some critical presence missions can only be achieved this way. Where a continuous presence is not required, periodic rotations offer a means to exercise and train with partner nations and to demonstrate the ability to rapidly deploy to a region. The demand for periodic rotations is likely to grow from both partner nations and combatant commanders because of their political and operational flexibility. That said, periodic rotations incur per-deployment movement costs similar to those experienced by units supporting continuous rotations.

If we are correct that demand for rotational forces is likely to remain high or grow, the USAF will need additional resources, alternative organizational structures, or new concepts to meet these demands. In our judgment, new rotational concepts (e.g., rotating permanently based forces within a theater, longer or shorter rotations, mixes of continuous and periodic presence) are particularly worth exploring in greater depth. Additional analysis would be valuable to identify the range of options and to assess their relative cost-effectiveness.

Global Posture for a Global Power

It appears that the debate about U.S. global posture has finally been joined. Much good can come from an open and thoughtful exploration of U.S. presence and access needs in the coming decades. Unfortunately, much of the current debate revolves around dangerous misperceptions. For example, some authors accuse long-time U.S. defense partners of freeriding on U.S. defense investments. Whatever the merits of arguments in favor of greater defense spending by particular partner nations, this line of argument misrepresents U.S. overseas military presence as one-sided, i.e., a gift to the host nation. In reality, these relationships have endured because of the considerable mutual benefits to both sides, including a wide range of security cooperation initiatives, increased regional stability, mutual support during contingencies, and, for the United States, the ability to conduct operations that would be infeasible without a global network of bases and partners. Americans take for granted the ability to project power globally, but this would not be possible without access to partner nation airfields, ports, and territory that often are not even in the immediate combat theater. For example, neither Operation Iraqi Freedom nor Enduring Freedom would have been possible without access to en route airfields and other support facilities in Spain, Italy, and Germany.

Another misperception is that great savings are to be found in cutting overseas forces and facilities.[192] Most of the Cold War global posture has already been dismantled. Although some additional savings are likely possible, fiscal benefits must be carefully weighed against the operational and strategic costs. For example, the USAF has only seven fighter wings deployed abroad (one in the UK, one in Germany, one in Italy, two in Korea, and two in Japan), and only one of these (the 48th Wing at RAF Lakenheath in the UK) is a full wing. The remaining six all require reinforcements from the United States to be at full strength. With changing strategic demands, it is appropriate to consider whether some realignment is called for among overseas locations, both within and across regions. That said, any major realignment risks hindering opportunities for training with our closest partners, may undermine relationships that have provided benefits for many decades, and could lead to the closure of bases that have proven their worth in past contingencies. Fewer forces and fewer bases ultimately translate into reduced

---

[192] See Lostumbo et al., RAND, 2013, for a detailed cost analysis of overseas basing options.

operational flexibility and could undermine U.S. regional stability, deterrence, and reassurance objectives.

Ultimately, the nation faces a critical choice: Do we intend to remain a global military power or not? There are substantial costs associated with either choice. If we choose the former, a large set of responsibilities and force demands flow from that decision and cannot be avoided. Global power necessitates a global force posture. It requires sustained and stable investment in human capital (our own and partners), forces, facilities, and relationships. These include developing and maintaining access relationships, forward bases, and forces; meeting security commitments to partner nations; sustaining a global transportation and communications network; and fielding forces capable of deploying globally and conducting effective military operations against a wide range of potential adversaries.

U.S. global posture is not the product of an overdeveloped sense of responsibility for other nations' security needs, but rather a prudent investment to protect U.S. interests. The fact that the United States has shared security interests with close partners in key regions is something to celebrate, not bemoan. The benefits in terms of opportunities for access and the ability to positively influence security in key regions far outweigh the costs of such commitments. That said, global posture should evolve to meet changing security demands, both in the nature and location of security threats. The future American global posture will feature a portfolio of arrangements and facilities, ranging from a small number of anchor bases in key nations to dozens of locations where its presence is modest and periodic. The Cold War global posture proved to be a strategic investment, serving the United States and its partners well for over 50 years. Current efforts to realign U.S. global posture into an increasingly agile and geographically diverse presence should likewise be viewed as a strategic investment, one that will pay benefits in ways unforeseen and over a time horizon likely measured in decades.

Bibliography

Adkin, Mark, *Urgent Fury: The Battle for Grenada*, Lexington, Mass.: Lexington Books, 1989.

Air Force Instruction 11-202, Vol. 3, *Flying Operations: General Flight Rules*, October 22, 2010. As of August 27, 2013:
http://www.e-publishing.af.mil/shared/media/epubs/AFI11-202V3.pdf

Air Force Pamphlet 10-1403, *Air Mobility Planning Factors*, December 12, 2013. As of August 27, 2013:
http://www.e-publishing.af.mil/shared/media/epubs/AFPAM10-1403.pdf

Air Mobility Command, *Air Mobility Command Global En Route Strategy White Paper*, Scott AFB, Illinois, July 2010.

AMC—*See* Air Mobility Command.

"AMC's Pacific En Route Posture," briefing slides, Scott AFB, Illinois: HQ Air Mobility Command, January 2013.

Armacost, Michael H., and Daniel I. Okimoto, eds., *The Future of America's Alliances with Northeast Asia*, Stanford, Calif.: Asia-Pacific Research Center, 2004.

Arteh, Abdourahim, "Djibouti Police Battle Crowds Protesting Election Result," Reuters, March 1, 2013.

AUSMIN 2010, Australia–United States Exchange of Letters Relating to Harold E. Holt Naval Communications Station Fact Sheet, November 8, 2010. As of August 27, 2013:
http://www.dfat.gov.au/geo/us/ausmin/Exchange-of-Letters-Relating-to-Harold-E.pdf

Australian Department of Defence, "Australia-U.S. Joint Combined Training Centre," July 8, 2004. As of August 27, 2013:
http://www.defence.gov.au/minister/Hilltpl.cfm?CurrentId=4016

Bacevich, Andrew J., *American Empire: The Realities and Consequences of U.S. Diplomacy*, Cambridge, Mass.: Harvard University Press, 2002.

Baker, Anni P., *American Soldiers Overseas: The Global Military Presence*, Westport, Conn.: Praeger Publishers, 2004.

Barnett, Michael N., *Dialogues in Arab Politics*, New York: Columbia University Press, 1998.

Barry, Ellen, "Georgia's President Concedes Defeat in Parliamentary Election," *New York Times*, October 2, 2012.

———, "With Visit, Russian Reinforces Its Custody of Islands, Angering Japan," *New York Times*, November 1, 2010.

Baum, Matthew A., and Philip B. K. Potter, "The Relationship Between Mass Media, Public Opinion, and Foreign Policy: Towards a Theoretical Synthesis," *Annual Review of Political Science*, Vol. 11, No. 39, 2008, pp. 39–65.

Bell, B. B., statement before the U.S. Senate Armed Services Committee, March 7, 2006.

Bello, Walden, "Moment of Decision: The Philippines, the Pacific, and the U.S. Bases," in, Joseph Gerson and Bruce Birchard, eds., *The Sun Never Sets: Confronting the Network of Foreign U.S. Military Bases*, Boston, Mass.: South End Press, 1991.

Benson, Lawrence R., *USAF Aircraft Basing in Europe, North Africa, and the Middle East, 1945–1980*, Ramstein Air Base, Germany: Office of History, Headquarters United States Air Forces in Europe, 1981, Declassified on July 20, 2011.

Berry, William E. Jr., *U.S. Bases in the Philippines: The Evolution of the Special Relationship*, Boulder, Colo.: Westview Press, 1989.

Blaker, James R., *The United States Overseas Basing: An Anatomy of the Dilemma*, New York: Praeger, 1990.

Blanchard, Christopher, *Qatar: Background and U.S. Relations*, Washington, D.C.: Congressional Research Service, 2012.

Bloomfield, Lincoln P., Jr., "Politics and Diplomacy of the Global Defense Posture Review," in Carnes Lord, ed., *Reposturing the Force: U.S. Overseas Presence in the Twenty-First Century*, Newport, R.I.: Naval War College Press, 2006.

Bowie, Christopher J., *The Anti-Access Threat and Theater Air Bases*, Washington, D.C.: Center for Strategic and Budgetary Assessments, 2002.

———, "The Lessons of Salty Demo," *Air Force Magazine*, March 2009, pp. 54–57. As of August 27, 2013:
http://www.airforce-magazine.com/MagazineArchive/Pages/2009/March%202009/0309salty.aspx

Boyne, Walter J., "El Dorado Canyon," *Air Force Magazine*, Vol. 82, No. 3, March 1999.

Brass, Jennifer N., "Djibouti's Unusual Resource Curse," *Journal of Modern African Studies*, Vol. 46, No. 4, 2008.

Breum, Martin, and Jorgen Chemnitz, "No, Greenland Does Not Belong to China," *New York Times*, February 20, 2013.

Bronson, Rachel, *Thicker Than Oil: America's Uneasy Partnership with Saudi Arabia*, Oxford, UK: Oxford University Press, 2008.

Calder, Kent E., *Embattled Garrisons: Competitive Base Politics and American Globalism*, Princeton, N.J.: Princeton University Press, 2007.

Calder, Kent, and Min Ye, *The Making of Northeast Asia*, Stanford, Calif.: Stanford University Press, 2010.

Call, Steve, *Selling Air Power: Military Aviation and American Popular Culture After World War II*, College Station, Tex.: Texas A&M University Press, 2009.

Camm, Frank, Lauren Caston, Alexander C. Hou, Forrest E. Morgan, and Alan J. Vick, *Managing Risk in USAF Force Planning*, Santa Monica, Calif.: RAND Corporation, MG-827-AF, 2009. As of August 27, 2013:
http://www.rand.org/pubs/monographs/MG827.html

Campbell, Kurt M., and Celeste Johnson Ward, "New Battle Stations?" *Foreign Affairs*, September/October 2003, pp. 95–99.

Cesar, Mike, "Rising Nationalism Threatens U.S. Anti-Drug Base in Ecuador," *World Politics Review*, April 30, 2008.

Chicago Council on Global Affairs, *Chicago Council on Global Affairs 2012 Poll*. As of August 27, 2013:
http://www.thechicagocouncil.org/UserFiles/File/Task%20Force%20Reports/2012_CCS_Report.pdf

Chiu, Daniel Y., and Jonathan T. Dworken, *The Political Effects of U.S. Military Presence in the Asian-Pacific Region*, Alexandria, Va.: Center for Naval Analyses, April 1991.

Clarke, Duncan L., and Daniel O'Connor, "U.S. Base Rights Payments After the Cold War," *Orbis*, Vol. 37, No. 3, Summer 1993.

Cliff, Roger, Mark Burles, Michael S. Chase, Derek Eaton, and Kevin L. Pollpeter, *Entering the Dragon's Lair: Chinese Antiaccess Strategies and Their Implications for the United States*, Santa Monica, Calif.: RAND Corporation, MG-524-AF, 2007. As of August 27, 2013:
http://www.rand.org/pubs/monographs/MG524.html

Clinton, Hillary Rodham, "Remarks at Press Availability," Hanoi, Vietnam, July 23, 2010. As of August 27, 2013:
http://www.state.gov/secretary/rm/2010/07/145095.htm

CNIC Naval Support Activity Bahrain website, "NSA Bahrain History," no date. As of August 27, 2013:
http://www.cnic.navy.mil/Bahrain/About/History/index.htm and http://www.cusnc.navy.mil/

Cohen, Michael, and James Hardy, "Philippines, U.S. Confirm U.S. Navy's Return to Subic Bay," *Jane's Online*, October 12, 2012. As of August 27, 2013:
http://www.janes.com/products/janes/defence-security-report.aspx?id=1065972334

Commission on Review of Overseas Military Facility Structure of the United States, Final Report, Washington, D.C., May 9, 2005.

Constello, John, *The Pacific War: 1941–1945*, New York: Harper Perennial, 1982.

Converse, Elliott V. III, *Circling the Earth: United States Plans for a Postwar Overseas Military Base System, 1942–1948*, Maxwell AFB, Ala.: Air University Press, 2005.

Cook, Malcolm, Raoul Heinrichs, Rory Medcalf, and Andrew Shearer, *Power and Choice: Asian Security Futures*, Australia: Lowy Institute for International Policy, 2010.

Cooley, Alexander, *Base Politics: Democratic Change and the U.S. Military Overseas*, Ithaca, N.Y.: Cornell University Press, 2008.

———, "Manas Hysteria: Why the United States Can't Keep Buying Off Kyrgyz Leaders to Keep Its Vital Air Base Open," *Foreignpolicy.com*, April 12, 2010. As of August 27, 2013: http://www.foreignpolicy.com/articles/2010/04/12/manas_hysteria

———, *Great Games, Local Rules; The New Great Power Contest in Central Asia*, Oxford, UK: Oxford University Press, 2012.

Cooley, Alexander, and Kimberly Marten, "Base Motives: The Political Economy of Okinawa's Antimilitarism," *Armed Forces and Society*, Vol. 32, No. 4, July 2006.

Cooley, Alexander, and Daniel H. Nexon, "Bahrain's Base Politics: The Arab Spring and America's Military Bases," *Foreignaffairs.com*, April 5, 2011.

Cooley, Alexander, and Hendrik Spruyt, *Contracting States: Sovereign Transfers in International Relations*, Princeton, N.J.: Princeton University Press, 2009.

Cordesman, Anthony H., *Bahrain, Oman, Qatar and the UAE, Challenges of Security*, Boulder, Colo.: Westview Press, 1997.

Cronin, Patrick M., Paul S. Giarra, Zachary M. Hosford, and Timothy A Walton, *Yokota: Civil-Military Use of U.S. Bases in Japan*, Washington, D.C.: Center for New American Security, 2012.

Davis, Lynn E., et al., *U.S. Overseas Military Presence: What Are the Strategic Choices?* Santa Monica, California: RAND, 2012, MG-1211-AF. As of August 27, 2013: http://www.rand.org/pubs/monographs/MG1211.html

De Castro, Renato C., "Philippine Defense Policy in the 21st Century: Autonomous Defense or Back to the Alliance?" *Pacific Affairs*, Vol. 78, No. 3, Fall 2005.

Defense Advisory Committee, *A New U.S. Defense Strategy for a New Era: Military Superiority, Agility and Efficiency*, Washington, D.C.: Stimson, 2012.

Defense Manpower Data Center, *Military Personnel Historical Reports, FY 1967*. As of August 27, 2013:
http://siadapp.dmdc.osd.mil/personnel/MILITARY/history/309hist.htm

————, *Active Duty Military Personnel Strengths by Regional Area and by Country*, September 30, 2010. As of August 27, 2013:
http://siadapp.dmdc.osd.mil/personnel/MILITARY/history/hst1009.pdf

Dempsey, Martin E., "Gen. Dempsey Briefs the Pentagon Press Corps," June 7, 2012. As of August 27, 2013:
http://www.jcs.mil/speech.aspx?id=1710

Duke, Simon, "U.S. Basing in Britain, 1945–1960," in Simon W. Duke and Wolfgang Krieger, eds., *U.S. Military Forces in Europe: The Early Years, 1945–1970*, Boulder, Colo.: Westview Press, 1993.

Dzyubenko, Olga, "Russian Ally Kyrgyzstan Set U.S. Air Base Closure Deadline," Reuters, June 20, 2013. As of August 27, 2013:
http://www.reuters.com/article/2013/06/20/us-kyrgyzstan-usa-base-idUSBRE95J0I620130620

Eaglen, Mackenzie "What's Likely in New Pentagon Strategy: 2 Theaters, Fewer Bases, A2AD," *Breaking Defense*, December 20, 2011. As of August 27, 2013:
http://breakingdefense.com/2011/12/20/whats-likely-in-new-pentagon-strategy-2-theaters-fewer-bases/

Ehrhard, Thomas P., *An Air Force Strategy for the Long Haul*, Washington, D.C.: Center for Strategic and Budgetary Assessments, 2009.

Ehrhard, Thomas P., and Robert O. Work, *Range, Persistence, Stealth, and Networking: The Case for A Carrier-Based Unmanned Combat Air System*, Washington, D.C.: Center for Strategic and Budgetary Assessments, 2008.

Feith, Douglas J., *Strengthening U.S. Global Defense Posture*, Report to Congress, Washington, D.C.: U.S. Department of Defense, September 2004.

Fitzgibbon, Joel, MP, Minister for Defence, "Minister for Defence Meeting with U.S. Secretary of Defense, Signing of Harold E. Holt Treaty," Canberra, Australia: Australian Ministry of Defense. As of August 27, 2013:
http://www.defence.gov.au/minister/70tpl.cfm?CurrentId=8000

Flanagan, Jr., *Battle for Panama: Inside Operation Just Cause*, Washington, D.C.: Brassey's, 1993.

Flournoy, Michele, and Janine Davidson, "Obama's New Global Posture: The Logic of U.S. Foreign Deployments," *Foreign Affairs*, Vol. 91, No. 4, July/August 2012, pp. 55–63.

Frelinger, David et al., "Assessing Options for Future USAF Force Posture in SWA," unpublished RAND briefing, August 2011.

Frickenstein, Scott G., "Kicked Out of K2," *Air Force Magazine*, Vol. 93, No. 9, September 2010.

Friedman, Benjamin H., and Justin Logan, "Why the U.S. Military Budget Is 'Foolish and Sustainable,'" *Orbis*, Vol. 56, No. 2, Spring 2012, pp. 179–183.

Galway, Lionel A., Mahyar A. Amouzegar, Richard J. Hillestad, and Don Snyder, *Reconfiguring Footprint to Speed Expeditionary Aerospace Forces Deployment*, Santa Monica, Calif.: RAND Corporation, MR-1625-AF, 2002. As of August 27, 2013: http://www.rand.org/pubs/monograph_reports/MR1625.html

Garamone, Jim, "U.S. Establishes Full-Time Aviation Detachment in Poland," *American Forces Press Service*, November 9, 2012.

Gellner, Ernest and John Breuilly, *Nations and Nationalism*, second edition, Ithaca, N.Y.: Cornell University Press, 2009

Gerson, Joseph, and Bruce Birchard, eds., *The Sun Never Sets: Confronting the Network of Foreign U.S. Military Bases*, Boston, Mass.: South End Press, 1991.

Gertler, Jeremiah, *Operation Odyssey Dawn (Libya): Background and Issues for Congress*, Washington, D.C.: Congressional Research Service Report R41725, March 28, 2011.

Gillem, Mark L., *America Town: Building the Outposts of Empire*, Minneapolis, Minn.: University of Minnesota Press, 2007.

Gleason, Gregory, "The Uzbek Expulsion of U.S. Forces and Realignment in Central Asia," *Problems of Post-Communism*, Vol. 53, No. 2, March/April 2006.

GlobalSecurity.org, "Eloy Alfaro Air Base/FOL Manta, Ecuador." As of August 27, 2013: http://www.globalsecurity.org/military/facility/manta.htm

Goldstein, Erik, Richard Langhome, and Michael Graham Fry, *Guide to International Relations and Diplomacy*, New York: Continuum International Publishing Group, 2004.

Gordon, Tomas F., *Historical Highlights of the First Twenty-Five Years of PACAF, 1957– 1981*, Hickam Air Force Base, Hawaii: Office of History Pacific Air Forces, July 30, 1982.

Gravois, Martha, "Military Families in Germany, 1946–1986: Why They Came and Why They Stayed," *Parameters*, Vol. 16, No. 4, 1986.

Green, Fred, *The Philippine Bases: Negotiating for the Future*, New York: Council on Foreign Relations, 1988.

Grimmett, Richard F., *U.S. Military Installations in NATO's Southern Region*, Washington, D.C.: U.S. Government Printing Office, 1986.

Gunzinger, Mark A., *Sustaining America's Strategic Advantage in Long-Range Strike*, Washington, D.C.: Center for Strategic and Budgetary Assessments, 2010.

Hagen, Jeff, and Jacob L. Heim, *U.S. Air Force Global Posture: Using Scenario Analysis to Identify Future Basing and Force Requirements*, Santa Monica, Calif.: RAND Corporation, RR-405-AF, forthcoming.

Hagen, Jeff, Patrick Mills, and Stephen M. Worman, *Analysis of Air Operations from Basing in Northern Australia*, Santa Monica, Calif.: RAND Corporation, TR-1306-AF, March 2013, not available to the general public.

Harkavy, Robert E., *Bases Abroad: The Global Foreign Military Presence*, New York: Oxford University Press, 1989.

———, "Thinking About Basing," *Naval War College Review*, Vol. 58, No. 3, Summer 2005.

Heller, David and Hans Lammerant, "U.S. Nuclear Weapons Bases in Europe," in Catherine Lutz ed., *The Bases of Empire: The Global Struggle Against U.S. Military Outposts*, London: Pluto Press, 2009.

Henry, Ryan, "Transforming the U.S. Global Defense Posture," *Naval War College Review*, Vol. 59, No. 2, Spring 2006, pp. 13–28.

Herring, George C., *From Colony to Superpower: U.S. Foreign Relations Since 1776*, New York: Oxford University Press, 2008

Hoehn, Andrew R., Adam Grissom, David A. Ochmanek, David A. Shlapak, and Alan J. Vick, *A New Division of Labor: Meeting America's Security Challenges Beyond Iraq*, Santa Monica, Calif.: RAND Corporation, MG-499-AF, 2007. As of August 27, 2013: http://www.rand.org/pubs/monographs/MG499.html

Holsti, Ole Rudolf, *Public Opinion and American Foreign Policy*, Revised Edition, Ann Arbor, Mich.: University of Michigan Press, 2004.

Huntington, Samuel P., *The Third Wave: Democratization in the Late Twentieth Century*, Norman, Okla.: University of Oklahoma Press, 1991.

Joint Chiefs of Staff, *The National Military Strategy of the United States 2011: Redefining America's Military Leadership*, Washington, D.C., 2011.

Joint Special Operations Task Force–Philippines, *JSOTF-P Mission*, Joint Special Operations Task Force Philippines website. As of August 27, 2013: http://jsotf-p.blogspot.com/

Joint Staff, "Global Defense Posture," unpublished background paper, April 16, 2012.

Kabashima, Ikuo, and Gill Steel, *Changing Politics in Japan*, Ithaca, N.Y.: Cornell University Press, 2010.

Kadena Air Base, 18th Wing History. As of August 27, 2013:
    http://www.kadena.af.mil/library/history/18thwinghistory.asp

Kalaitzidis, Akis, and Nikolaos Zahariadis, "Papandreou's NATO Policy: Continuity or Change?" *Journal of the Hellenic Diaspora*, Vol. 23, No. 1, 1997.

Katzenstein, Peter J., *A World of Regions: Asia and Europe in the American Imperium*, Ithaca, N.Y.: Cornell University Press, 2005.

Katzman, Kenneth, *The United Arab Emirates (UAE): Issues for U.S. Policy*, Washington, D.C.: Congressional Research Service, October 4, 2012.

Kowert, Paul, and Jeffery Legro, "Norms, Identity, and Their Limits: A Theoretical Reprise," in Peter J. Katzenstein, ed., *The Culture of National Security: Norms and Identity in World Politics*, New York: Columbia University Press, 1996.

Krasner, Stephen D., *Sovereignty: Organized Hypocrisy*, Princeton: Princeton University Press, 1999.

Krepinevich, Andrew F., *Seven Deadly Scenarios: A Military Futurist Explores War in the 21st Century*, New York: Bantam, 2009.

———, *Why AirSea Battle?* Washington, D.C.: Center for Strategic and Budgetary Assessments, 2010.

Krepinevich, Andrew F., and Robert O. Work, *A New Global Defense Posture for the Second Transoceanic Era*, Washington, D.C.: Center for Strategic and Budgetary Assessments, 2007.

Krutky, Judy, "Can/Should the U.S. Base on Diego Garcia be Maintained? Background and Current Positions of Key Stakeholders," unpublished manuscript, December 2012.

Kunsan Air Base website. As of August 27, 2013:
    http://www.kunsan.af.mil/library/wolfpackheritage/airbase.asp

Lambeth, Benjamin S., *Air Power Against Terror: America's Conduct of Operation Enduring Freedom*, Santa Monica, Calif.: RAND Corporation, 2005. As of August 27, 2013:
    http://www.rand.org/pubs/monographs/MG166-1.html

Lang, Thomas, *Defining and Evaluating Reliable Options for Overseas Combat Support Basing*, Santa Monica, Calif.: Pardee RAND Graduate School, dissertation, RGSD-250, 2009. As of August 27, 2013:
    http://www.rand.org/pubs/rgs_dissertations/RGSD250.html

Larrabee, F. Stephen, "Athens: Greece for the Greeks," *Foreign Policy*, Vol. 45, Winter 1981–1982.

Leffler, Melvyn P., "The American Conception of National Security and the Beginnings of the Cold War, 1945–48," *The American Historical Review*, Vol. 89, No. 2, April 1984.

———, *A Preponderance of Power: National Security, the Truman Administration, and the Cold War*, Stanford, Calif.: Stanford University Press, 1993.

Linz, Juan J., and Alfred Stepan, "Toward Consolidated Democracies," *Journal of Democracy*, Vol. 7, No. 2, 1996.

Lipson, Charles, *Reliable Partners: How Democracies Have Made a Separate Peace*, Princeton, N.J.: Princeton University Press, 2003.

Lockheed Martin, "Lockheed Martin Receives $3 Million Contract to Continue Study of Air-Launched PAC-3 Missiles," press release, January 16, 2007. As of August 27, 2013:
http://www.lockheedmartin.com/us/news/press-releases/2007/january/LockheedMartinReceives3MillionContr.html

Logan, Samuel, "U.S. Faces Eviction from Ecuadorian Base," *ISN Security Watch*, January 12, 2007. As of August 27, 2013:
http://www.isn.ethz.ch/isn/Digital-Library/Articles/Detail/?ots591=4888caa0-b3db-1461-98b9-e20e7b9c13d4&lng=en&id=51840

Lord, Carnes, ed., *Reposturing the Force: U.S. Overseas Presence in the Twenty-first Century*, Newport, R.I.: Naval War College Press, February 2006. As of August 27, 2013:
http://www.usnwc.edu/Publications/Naval-War-College-Press/Newport-Papers/Documents/26-pdf.aspx

Lostumbo, Michael, Michael J. McNerney, Eric Peltz, Derek Eaton, David R. Frelinger, Victoria A. Greenfield, John Halliday, Patrick Mills, Bruce R. Nardulli, Stacie L. Pettyjohn, Jerry M. Sollinger, and Stephen Worman, *Overseas Basing of U.S. Military Forces: An Assessment of Relative Costs and Strategic Benefits*, Santa Monica, Calif.: RAND Corporation, RR-201-OSD, 2013. As of August 27, 2013:
http://www.rand.org/pubs/research_reports/RR201.html

Loulis, John C., "Papandreou's Foreign Policy," *Foreign Affairs*, Vol. 63, No. 2, Winter 1984.

Louis, William Roger, *Imperialism at Bay*, New York: Oxford University Press, 1978.

Lum, Thomas, *The Republic of the Philippines and U.S. Interests*, Washington, D.C.: Congressional Research Service, April 5, 2012.

Lundestad, Geir, "Empire by Invitation? The United States and Western Europe, 1945–1952," *Journal of Peace Research*, Vol. 23, No. 3, September 1986, pp. 263–277.

Lunn, Jon, "The Chagos Islanders," London, UK: Library House of Commons, April 20, 2012.

Lutz, Catherine, ed., *The Bases of Empire: The Global Struggle Against U.S. Military Outposts*, London: Pluto Press, 2009.

Lynch, Marc, "Paint by Numbers," *The National*, May 29, 2009. As of August 27, 2013: http://www.thenational.ae/news/world/middle-east/paint-by-numbers#full

Mansfield, Edward D., and Jack Snyder, *Electing to Fight: Why Emerging Democracies Go to War*, Cambridge, Mass.: MIT Press, 2005.

Manyin, Mark E, Emma Chanlett-Avery, and Mary Beth Nikitin, *U.S.-South Korea Relations,* Washington, D.C.: Congressional Research Service, November 28, 2011.

Martin, Lisa L., *Democratic Commitments: Legislatures and International Cooperation*, Princeton, N.J.: Princeton University Press, 2000.

Mason, R. Chuck, *Status of Forces Agreement (SOFA): What Is It, and How Has It Been Utilized?* Washington, D.C.: Congressional Research Service, January 5, 2011.

Mills, Patrick, Adam Grissom, Jennifer Kavanagh, Leila Mahnad, and Stephen M. Worman, *A Cost Analysis of the U.S. Air Force Overseas Posture: Informing Strategic Choices*, Santa Monica, Calif.: RAND Corporation, RR-150-AF, 2013. As of August 27, 2013: http://www.rand.org/pubs/research_reports/RR150.html

Mochizuki, Mike, and Michael O'Hanlon, "Solving the Okinawa Problem: How Many Marines Do We Still Need in Japan?" *Foreign Policy*, October 12, 2012.

Monteleone, Carla, "The Evolution of the Euro-Atlantic Pluralistic Security Community: Impact and Perspectives of the Presence of American Bases in Italy," *Journal of Transatlantic Studies*, Vol. 5, No. 1, 2007.

Moroney, Jennifer D. P., Patrick H. Mills, David T. Orletsky, and David E. Thaler, *Working with Allies and Partners: A Cost-Based Analysis of U.S. Air Forces in Europe*, Santa Monica, Calif.: RAND Corporation, TR-1241-AF, 2012. As of August 27, 2013: http://www.rand.org/pubs/technical_reports/TR1241.html

Munoz, Carlo, "Panetta Says Pentagon Will Drop Base Closure Plans for Fiscal Year 2013," *DEFCON Hill: The HILL's Defense Blog*, August 6, 2012. As of August 27, 2013: http://thehill.com/blogs/defcon-hill/budget-appropriations/242385-dod-drops-base-realignment-plan-for-fiscal-2013-

———, "The Philippines Re-Opens Military Bases to U.S. Forces," *DEFCON Hill*, June 6, 2012. As of August 27, 2013: http://thehill.com/blogs/defcon-hill/operations/231257-philippines-re-opens-military-bases-to-us-forces-

Nalty, Bernard C., ed., *Winged Shield, Winged Sword: A History of the United States Air Force*, Volume II, *1950–1997*, Washington, D.C.: U.S. Air Force, 1997.

National Air and Space Intelligence Center, *China: Connecting the Dots—Strategic Challenges Posed by a Re-Emergent Power*, Wright-Patterson AFB, Ohio, 2007.

Nichol, Jim, *Kyrgyzstan: Recent Developments and U.S. Interests*, Washington, D.C.: Congressional Research Service, January 19, 2012.

Nicholson, Brendan, "U.S. Forces Get Nod to Share Our Bases," *The Australian National Affairs*, November 6, 2010. As of August 27, 2013: http://www.theaustralian.com.au/national-affairs/us-forces-get-nod-to-share-our-bases/story-fn59niix-1225948576258

O'Donnell, Guillermo, and Philippe Schmitter, "Tentative Conclusions About Uncertain Democracies," in Guillermo O'Donnell, Philippe Schmitter, and Laurence Whitehead, eds., *Transitions from Authoritarian Rule*, Part 4, Baltimore, Md.: Johns Hopkins University Press.

Office of the President of the Philippines, "The 1987 Constitution of the Republic of the Philippines – Article XVIII," the *Official Gazette Online*.

Office of the Secretary of Defense, *Report to Congress: Kosovo/Operation Allied Force After-Action Report,* Washington, D.C.: U.S. Department of Defense, January 31, 2000.

———, *Annual Report on the Military Power of the People's Republic of China 2002*, Washington, D.C.: U.S. Department of Defense, 2002. As of August 27, 2013: http://www.defense.gov/news/Jul2002/d20020712china.pdf

———, *Annual Report to Congress: Military and Security Developments Involving the People's Republic of China 2010*, Washington, D.C.: Department of Defense, 2010. As of August 27, 2013: http://www.defense.gov/pubs/pdfs/2010_CMPR_Final.pdf

———, *Sustaining U.S. Global Leadership: Priorities for 21st Century Defense*, Washington, D.C.: Department of Defense, January 2012

O'Hanlon, Michael, *Unfinished Business: U.S. Overseas Military Presence in the 21st Century*, Washington, D.C.: Center for New American Security, 2008.

———, *The Wounded Giant: America's Armed Forces in an Age of Austerity*, NY: Penguin Press, 2011.

Overseas Basing Commission, *Report to the President and U.S. Congress*, Washington, D.C.: Commission on Review of Overseas Military Facility Structure of the United States, May 9, 2005.

Palyan, Hrair, *Lessons Learned, Operation Odyssey Dawn*, Ellsworth AFB, South Dakota: 28th Bomb Wing Public Affairs, March 21, 2012. As of August 27, 2013: http://www.ellsworth.af.mil/news/story.asp?id=123294757

Pargeter, Alison, *Libya the Rise and Fall of Qaddafi,* New Haven, Conn.: Yale University Press, 2012.

Peterson Air Force Base website, "Description of 821st Air Base Group, Thule AB, Greenland Mission." As of August 27, 2013:
http://www.peterson.af.mil/units/821stairbase/index.asp

Pettyjohn, Stacie L., *U.S. Global Defense Posture, 1783–2011*, Santa Monica, Calif.: RAND Corporation, MG-1244-AF, 2012. As of August 27, 2013:
http://www.rand.org/pubs/monographs/MG1244.html

Pettyjohn, Stacie L., and Alan J. Vick, "Okinawa Remains an Intractable Thorn for U.S. and Japan," *Asia Times Online*, May 25, 2012. As of August 27, 2013:
http://www.atimes.com/atimes/Japan/NE25Dh01.html

Pew Research Center, "Support for War in Afghanistan," Key Indicators Database, polling data, undated. As of August 27, 2013:
http://pewglobal.org/database/?indicator=9&mode=chart.

———, *Global Unease with Major World Powers: 47-Nation Pew Global Attitudes Survey*, Washington, D.C., June 27, 2007. As of August 27, 2013:
http://pewglobal.org/files/pdf/256.pdf

Pinter, William E., *Concentrating on Dispersed Operations: Answering the Emerging Antiaccess Challenge in the Pacific Rim*, Maxwell AFB, Ala.: Air University Press, April 2007.

Posen, Barry R., "Pull Back: the Case for a Less Activist Foreign Policy," *Foreign Affairs*, Vol. 91, No. 1, January/February 2013.

Prados, Alfred B., *Iraq: Former and Recent Military Confrontations*, Washington, D.C.: Congressional Research Service, October 16, 2002.

Public Law 110-181, National Defense Authorization Act for Fiscal Year 2008, February 21, 2008.

Puddington, Arch, *Freedom in the World 2013: Democratic Breakthroughs in the Balance*, 2013. As of August 27, 2013:
http://www.freedomhouse.org/sites/default/files/FIW%202013%20Booklet%20-%20for%20Web_0.pdf

Putnam, Robert D., "Diplomacy and Domestic Politics: the Logic of Two-Level Games," *International Organization*, Vol. 42, No. 3, Summer 1988.

Randolph, R. Sean, *The United States and Thailand: Alliance Dynamics, 1950–1985*, Berkley, Calif.: Institute of East Asian Studies, University of California, 1986.

Reilly, James, *Strong Society, Smart State: The Rise of Public Opinion in China's Japan Policy*, New York: Columbia University Press, 2011.

Risse-Kappen, Thomas, "Collective Identity in a Democratic Community: The Case of NATO," in Peter J. Katzenstein, ed., *The Culture of National Security: Norms and Identity in World Politics*, New York: Columbia University Press, 1996.

Roberts, Steven V., "Greece to Allow Most U.S. Bases," *New York Times*, December 13, 1974.

Rohter, Larry, "U.S. Accord With Panama on troops Hits a Snag," *New York Times*, April 26, 1998.

Romero, Simon, "Ecuador's Leader Purges Military and Moves to Expel American Base," *New York Times*, April 21, 2008.

Sand, Peter H., *United States and Britain in Diego Garcia: The Future of a Controversial Base*, New York: Palgrave Macmillan, 2009.

Sandars, Christopher, *America's Overseas Garrisons: The Leasehold Empire*, Oxford, N.Y.: Oxford University Press, 2000.

Scobell, Andrew, *China's Use of Military Force: Beyond the Great Wall and the Long March*, New York: Cambridge University Press, 2003.

Sharp, Walter, Statement before the House Armed Services Committee, April 6, 2011.

Sherry, Michael S., *Preparing for the Next War: American Plans for Postwar Defense*, 1941–45, New Haven, Conn.: Yale University Press, 1977.

Shlapak, David A., Toy I. Reid, Murray Scot Tanner, and Barry Wilson, *A Question of Balance: Political Context and Military Aspects of the China-Taiwan Dispute*, Santa Monica, Calif.: RAND Corporation, MG-888-SRF, 2009. As of August 27, 2013:
http://www.rand.org/pubs/monographs/MG888.html

Shlapak, David A., John Stillion, Olga Oliker, and Tanya Charlick-Paley, *A Global Access Strategy for the U.S. Air Force*, Santa Monica, Calif.: RAND Corporation, MR-1216-AF, 2002. As of August 27, 2013:
http://www.rand.org/pubs/monograph_reports/MR1216.html

Shlapak, David A., and Alan Vick, *Check Six Begins on the Ground: Responding to the Evolving Great Threat to U.S. Air Force Bases*, Santa Monica, Calif.: RAND Corporation, MR-606-AF, 1995. As of August 27, 2013:
http://www.rand.org/pubs/monograph_reports/MR606.html

Siegel, Adam B., *Basing and Other Constraints on Ground-Based Aviation Contributions to U.S. Contingency Operations*, Washington, D.C.: Center for Naval Analysis, March 1995.

Siegel, Matt, "As Part of Pact, U.S. Marines Arrive in Australia, in China's Strategic Backyard," *New York Times*, April 4, 2012.

Smith, Henry Ladd, *Airways Abroad: The Story of American World Air Routes*, Madison, Wisc.: The University of Wisconsin Press, 1950.

Smith, Perry McCoy, *The Air Force Plans for Peace: 1943–1945*, Baltimore, Md.: The Johns Hopkins Press, 1970.

Smith, Stephen, "Remarks to the Australian Strategic Policy Institute (ASPI), Australia's Changing Circumstances." August 1, 2012. As of August 27, 2013:
http://www.minister.defence.gov.au/2012/08/01/minister-for-defence-to-the-australian-strategic-policy-institute-aspi-australias-changing-strategic-circumstances/

Snyder, Jack, *Myths of Empire: Domestic Politics and International Ambition*, Ithaca, N.Y.: Cornell University Press, 1993.

———, *From Voting to Violence: Democratization and Nationalist Conflict*, New York: W. W. Norton & Company, 2000.

Snyder, Jack, and Karen Ballentine, "Nationalism and the Marketplace of Ideas," *International Security*, Vol. 21, No. 2, Fall 1996.

Snyder, Thomas S., and Daniel F. Harrington, *Historical Highlights United States Air Forces in Europe 1942–1997*, Ramstein Air Base, Germany: USAFE Office of History, March 14, 1997.

Spaatz, Carl A., "Air Power in the Atomic Age," *Collier's*, December 8, 1945.

Stambuk, George, "Foreign Policy and the Stationing of American Forces Abroad," *The Journal of Politics*, Vol. 25, No. 3, August 1963.

Sturm, Thomas, *USAF Overseas Forces and Bases: 1947–1967*, Washington, D.C.: Office of Air Force History, March 1969.

Sullivan, Kevin, "Romanians Eager for Long-Awaited Arrival of Yanks," *Washington Post*, February 6, 2006.

Thomason, James S., Robert J. Atwell, Robert Bovey, William E. Cralley, James Delaney, Michael P. Fischerkeller, Kongdan Oh Hassig, Charles Hawkins, and Gene Porter, *Transforming US Overseas Military Presence: Evidence and Options for DoD*, Volume 1: *Main Report*, Institute for Defense Analyses (IDA), Paper P-3707, July 2002.

U.S. Air Force, *United States Air Force Statistical Digest*, Washington, D.C.: Headquarters Air Force, multiple years.

———, "Global Strike Command Supports Operation Odyssey Dawn," Barksdale AFB, Louisiana: Air Force Global Strike Command Public Affairs, March 20, 2011. As of August 27, 2013:
http://www.afgsc.af.mil/news/story.asp?id=123247722

———, "B-52 Stratofortress," online fact sheet, September 20, 2005. As of August 27, 2013:
http://www.af.mil/AboutUs/FactSheets/Display/tabid/224/Article/104465/b-52-stratofortress.aspx

U.S. Central Intelligence Agency, *The CIA World Factbook: Virgin Islands*, no date. As of August 27, 2013:
https://www.cia.gov/library/publications/the-world-factbook/geos/vq.html

U.S. Department of Defense, *Strengthening U.S. Global Defense Posture*, report to Congress, Washington, D.C., September 2004.

———, *Base Structure Report: Fiscal Year 2010 Baseline.* As of August 27, 2013:
http://www.acq.osd.mil/ie/download/bsr/bsr2010baseline.pdf

———, *Sustaining U.S. Global Leadership: Priorities for 21st Century Defense*, Washington, D.C., January 2012.

U.S. Department of State, "Greece: Profile," no date. As of August 27, 2013:
http://www.state.gov/outofdate/bgn/greece/73825.htm

———, "Toward a Deeper Alliance: United States–Philippines Bilateral Cooperation," online fact sheet, January 27, 2012. As of August 27, 2013:
http://www.state.gov/r/pa/prs/ps/2012/01/182689.htm

———, *Joint Defense Facility at Pine Gap: Agreement Between the United States of America and Australia signed at Canberra*, June 4, 1998. As of August 27, 2013:
http://www.state.gov/documents/organization/112459.pdf

U.S. Fish and Wildlife Service, "Pacific Remote Islands Marine National Monument," last updated April 5, 2011. As of August 27, 2013:
http://www.fws.gov/pacificremoteislandsmarinemonument/

U.S. General Accounting Office, *Drug Control: International Counterdrug Sites Being Developed*, Washington, D.C., December 2000. As of August 27, 2013:
http://www.gao.gov/products/GAO-01-63BR

U.S. Geological Survey, *Navassa Island: A Photographic Tour*, August 2000. As of January 24, 2013:
http://coastal.er.usgs.gov/navassa/

U.S. Government Accountability Office, *Force Structure: Improved Cost Information and Analysis Needed to Guide Overseas Military Posture Decisions*, Report to the Committee on Armed Services, U.S. Senate, Washington, D.C.: June 2012.

U.S. House of Representatives, *Making Emergency Supplemental Appropriations for the Fiscal Year Ending September 30, 2005, and for Other Purposes*, Conference Report 109-72, Washington, D.C., 2005.

————, U.S. House of Representatives, *Mystery at Manas: Strategic Blind Spots in the Department of Defense's Fuel Contracts In Kyrgyzstan*, Washington, D.C.: Report of the Majority Staff, Subcommittee on National Security and Foreign Affairs, Committee on Oversight and Government, December 2010.

U.S. Navy, *Report to Congress on Camp Lemonnier, Djibouti Master Plan*, Washington, D.C.: Department of the Navy, August 2012.

"U.S. Reps Paul, Kucinich Urge Military Pullout from Japan Amid Budget Woes," *The Japan Times*, February 17, 2011.

U.S. Senate, *The Gulf Security Architecture: Partnership with the Gulf Cooperation Council*, a majority staff report prepared for the use of the Committee on Foreign Relations, United States Senate, One Hundred Twelfth Congress, Second Session, Washington, D.C.: U.S. Government Printing Office, June 19, 2012.

Van Tol, Jan, Mark Gunzinger, Andrew Krepinevich, and Jim Thomas, *AirSea Battle: A Point-of-Departure Operational Concept*, Washington, D.C.: Center for Strategic and Budgetary Assessments, 2010.

Van Zandt, John Parker, *Civil Aviation and Peace*, Washington, D.C.: The Brookings Institution, 1944.

————, *The Geography of World Air Transport*, Washington, D.C.: The Brookings Institution, 1944.

Vandiver, John, "US Seeking Extension of Manas Air Base Lease," *Stars and Stripes*, January 16, 2013.

Vick, Alan J., and Jacob L. Heim, *Assessing U.S. Air Force Basing Options in East Asia*, Santa Monica, Calif.: RAND Corporation, MG-1204-AF, January 2013, not available to the general public.

Vinas, Angel, "Negotiating the U.S.-Spanish Agreements, 1953–1988: A Spanish Perspective," *Jean Monnet/Robert Schuman Paper Series*, Vol. 3, No. 7, September 2003.

Vine, David, *Island of Shame: The Secret History of the U.S. Military Base on Diego Garcia*, Princeton, N.J.: Princeton University Press, 2009.

Vine, David, and Laura Jeffery, "'Give Us back Diego Garcia': Unity and Division Among Activists in the Indian Ocean," in Catherine Lutz ed., *The Bases of Empire: The Global Struggle Against U.S. Military Outposts*, London: Pluto Press, 2009.

Walt, Stephen, *The Origins of Alliances*, Ithaca, N.Y.: Cornell University Press, 1987.

Walt, Stephen M., "Why Alliances Endure or Collapse," *Survival*, Vol. 39, No. 1, 1997.

Webb, Katharine, *Are the Overseas Bases Worth the Bucks? An Approach to Assessing Operational Value and an Application to the Philippines*, Santa Monica, Calif.: RAND Corporation, RGSD-108, 1993. As of August 27, 2013:
http://www.rand.org/pubs/rgs_dissertations/RGSD108.html

Webbe, Stephen, "US Ponders Possible Loss of Military Bases in Greece," *Christian Science Monitor*, October 20, 1981.

Weller, George, *Bases Overseas*, New York: Harcourt, Brace and Company, 1944.

Wolf, Jim, "U.S. Plans 10-Month Warship Deployment to Singapore," *Reuters Online*, May 10, 2012. As of August 27, 2013:
http://www.reuters.com/article/2012/05/10/us-usa-singapore-warship-idUSBRE8481IE20120510

Woodley, Naomi, "Smith: No US bases in Australia," *ABC News*, August 2, 2012. As of August 27, 20133:
http://www.abc.net.au/am/content/2012/s3558731.htm

Yee, Andy, "U.S. Deployment of Littoral Combat Ships to Singapore," *East Asia Forum*. As of November 18, 2011:
http://www.eastasiaforum.org/2011/07/21/us-deployment-of-littoral-combat-ships-to-singapore/

Yeo, Andrew, "Not in Anyone's Backyard: The Emergence and Identity of a Transnational Anti-Base Network," *International Studies Quarterly*, Vol. 53, 2009.

———, "U.S. Military Base Realignment in South Korea," *Peace Review: A Journal of Social Justice*, Vol. 22, No. 2, May 2010a, pp. 113–120.

———, "Ideas and Institutions in Contentious Politics: Anti-U.S. Base Movements in Ecuador and Italy," *Comparative Politics*, Vol. 42, No. 4, July 2010b, pp. 441–446.

———, *Activists, Alliances, and Anti-U.S. Base Protests*, Cambridge: Cambridge University Press, 2011.

Zenko, Micah, *Between Threats and War: U.S. Discrete Military Operations in the Post–Cold War World*, Stanford, Calif.: Stanford University Press, 2010.